The Logic of Intuitive Decision Making

THE LOGIC OF INTUITIVE DECISION MAKING
A Research-Based Approach for Top Management

WESTON H. AGOR

Foreword by Ken Blanchard

Quorum Books

New York
Westport, Connecticut
London

Library of Congress Cataloging-in-Publication Data

Agor, Weston, H., 1939-
  The logic of intuitive decision making.

  Bibliography: p.
  Includes index.
  1. Decision-making. 2. Intuition (Psychology).
I. Title.
HD30.23.A35 1986   658.4'03   86–8119
ISBN: 0–89930–177–0 (lib. bdg. : alk. paper)

Library of Congress Catalog Card Number: 86–8119
ISBN: 0–89930–177–0

First published in 1986 by Quorum Books

Greenwood Press, Inc.
88 Post Road West, Westport, Connecticut 06881

Printed in the United States of America

The paper used in this book complies with the
Permanent Paper Standard issued by the National
Information Standards Organization (Z39.48–1984).

10 9 8 7 6 5 4 3 2 1

Copyright Acknowledgments

The author gratefully acknowledges permission to use portions of the following copyrighted material:

Excerpts from *Awakening Intuition* by Frances E. Vaughan. Copyright © 1979 by Frances E. Vaughan. Reprinted by permission of Doubleday & Company, Inc.

"Managing Brain Skills to Increase Productivity," by Weston H. Agor in *Public Administration Review* (November-December 1985). Reprinted with permission from *Public Administration Review* © 1985 by The American Society for Public Administration, 1120 G Street, N.W., Suite 500, Washington, D.C. All rights reserved.

Intuitive Management: Integrated Left and Right Brain Management Skills by Weston H. Agor. © Weston H. Agor. Reprinted by permission of the publisher, Prentice-Hall, Inc., Englewood Cliffs, N.J.

Reprinted, by permission of the publisher, from "The Logic of Intuition: How Top Executives Make Important Decisions," by Weston H. Agor, *Organizational Dynamics*, Winter 1986 © 1986 Periodicals Division, American Management Association, New York. All rights reserved.

William G. McGinnis, "Decision-Making Process," and Randolph J. Forrester, from the "Commentary" page, *Public Management* 65, 2 (February 1983), p. 17. Reprinted from *Public Management* magazine, February 1983, by special permission © 1983, International City Management Association, Washington, D.C.

To my father,
my late brother, and
my sons, Lawrence and William.

Contents

PART III: AGENDA FOR FUTURE RESEARCH

List of Exhibits

Foreword

Reading Weston Agor's book *The Logic of Intuitive Decision Making: A Research Based Approach for Top Management* really warmed my heart. One of the things that really "bugged" me during my ten years as a full time university professor was the "much ado about nothin'" research that was being done in my field of organizational behavior. Not only did you need a Ph.D. in statistics to understand most of it, but when you finally waded through it rarely did the research have any practical value to managers in the real world who were being bombarded daily with decisions that had to be made "yesterday."

Elton Mayo, the father of the human relations movement, had even gone so far in 1942 as saying that psychology, sociology, political science, and all the other social and behavioral sciences were unsuccessful as compared to physics, chemistry, biology, and the other natural and physical sciences. The reason was that when the soft sciences were taught students learned only factual or theoretical knowledge. Very little, if any, knowledge of acquaintance was taught—the ability to use the fact and theory learned to solve real life problems. Whereas in the successful sciences like chemistry or physics, for example, a student might be lectured to in the morning but most assuredly that student would be in a laboratory that afternoon where he or she was forced to apply and use what was learned in the morning to solve a problem. On the other hand, students in the social and behavioral sciences were often blindly taught one fact and theory after another fact and theory after another fact and theory. It was for this very reason that Mayo argued that our technical skills in this country are so much more advanced than our human skills. We are great at building machines but lousy at getting along with other human beings. When John Naisbitt wrote about the "high tech—high touch" trend forty years later in his best selling book *Megatrends* he suggested an even greater need today to close this gap between our technology and our humanness.

This is a long-winded way of saying that Weston Agor's book on intuitive decision making is worth reading. First of all, it is based on research—extensive research over a four-year period (1981–1985) with over 3000 executives from all kinds of organizations and settings. Second, he takes something like intuition, which has been called a ''non-rational'' skill by psychologists and academicians, and shows that it is really a very rational and logical decision making skill. Practicing managers have known for years that intuition—a kind of second sense—is a useful skill in making decisions but were afraid to mention it for fear they would be attacked as irrational thinkers. Thanks, Weston, you have really helped us out. Third, not only does Agor teach us in this book what intuition is and its importance, but he shows the reader how ''step-by-step you can *learn* to use and *develop* [italics mine] your intuitive ability for guiding key decisions—whether they be at work or in your personal life.'' And then, finally, Agor closes the loop in the last section of the book and makes ''recommendations for the direction future research on intuition should take if the results are to be *useful* [italics mine] to the world of applied management.''

All in all, I really liked this book and so will you. There is no doubt in my mind that the effective use of intuition in management can help improve the quality of decision making in organizations. All those left brain analytical techniques such as MBO, PERT, and economic forecasting models are just that— very logical and analytical. When it comes to intuition, one of my favorite quotes says it all: ''Of all the virtues—love, hope, and charity, the greatest of them all is common sense.'' Thanks, Weston, for helping us recognize and validate our using intuition to make a difference in our lives and the lives of people with whom we work and live.

Ken Blanchard
Co-author, *The One Minute Manager*

Preface

When I first started serious field research on the use of intuition in management in 1981, many of my professional colleagues thought I had surely lost my mind. They could not imagine what relevance intuition could possibly have to the process of decision making in modern organizations. At this writing, many of these same colleagues now say my research is the beginning of "a new wave." So much for "experts"!

This is the message of this book. Actively seek input and advice from all the sources you possibly can before making a key decision. Keep yourself open to these cues. But in the final analysis, you must make the decision *based on how you feel. You must trust yourself!*

This book tells you how to use your intuition to help make key decisions at work and in your personal life. What I have to recommend to you is what successful executives have taught me about how they use intuition to help guide their most important decisions. It also outlines steps you can take to develop your present intuitive ability further, and how you can join or establish an "intuition network" worldwide to promote the use of this skill in your own organization.

The book is divided into three major parts. The first part is what I call "The Logic of Intuitive Decision Making." It is the field research base upon which I derive much of what I have to recommend to you for use in the balance of the book. Chapter 1 outlines why intuition is becoming such an important management skill in organizations today, and why this will become more so in the decade just ahead. This chapter also defines in some detail what intuition is, and suggests that it is a very rational and logical decision making skill rather than a "non-rational" skill as it is often characterized by many psychologists and academicians.

Chapter 2 summarizes the highlights from field testing I conducted during the period 1981–85 among over 3,000 executives nationally in a wide variety of private and public sector organizations and management settings. One of the key

findings I report is that top executives in every organization studied are significantly different (statistically) from their subordinates in one key characteristic—
their ability to use intuition to make management decisions.[1] Based on this
startling finding, I proceeded to carry out a follow-up study in 1984–85 among
those executives who scored in the top 10 percent on my intuition survey instrument.[2] I wanted to determine if these top executives actually used their
intuitive ability to guide their most important management decisions. If so, I
wanted to find out how this process(es) worked—in part so that I could pass this
information on to you for your own use (see Chapter 3).

The second part of the book is "Implementing a Program for Using and
Developing Intuition to Increase Organizational Productivity." The three chapters contained here are based on what I learned from testing and personally
interviewing the executive samples discussed in Part I of the book. The key
objective of this section of the book is to show you how step-by-step you can
learn to use and develop your intuitive ability for guiding key decisions—whether
they be at work or in your personal life. Chapter 4 begins with you. Here I
outline ways you can go about exploring your intuitive ability—from formal
testing to other exercises and techniques. You are also provided with benchmark
data so that you can compare your level of intuitive ability to that of national
norms established through my national survey. Chapter 5 carries you one step
further beyond simply working with yourself to actually implementing a program
within the organization you presently work with. This program is designed to integrate the use and development of intuitive skills into the processes of management decision making on a regular basis. This chapter not only tells you how to
carry out such a program step-by-step with examples from leading private and
public sector organizations, but it also gives you several exercises to practice at
both an individual and an organizational level in doing so. Chapter 6 then describes in detail how a program designed to implement what you have just learned
actually works to help increase personal and organizational productivity. Two
case studies are examined—one from the private sector (Tenneco, Inc.) and one
from the public sector (the City of Phoenix) based on workshops I conducted for
them.

The last part of the book outlines briefly an "Agenda for Future Research."
Here in Chapter 7 I conclude with recommendations for the direction future
research on intuition should take if the results are to be useful to the world of
applied management as well as generate financial support for ongoing work in
this field.

In the appendix, you will also find other helpful materials. The first item there
is an outline of a "model intuition program" you can review for possible implementation in your own organization. Forms for establishing an "intuition
network" within your organization and also for joining a "global intuition network" in order to share and develop your intuitive talent more effectively are
also provided there. Finally, you will find a copy of the original open-ended

questionnaire that was employed to explore how highly intuitive executives actually use their ability to make important decisions.

At the end of the book, I have provided an extensive annotated bibliography that can serve as a resource guide in helping you to use and develop your intuitive ability further. The bibliography is divided into two main sections, "Using and Developing Your Intuitive Brain Skills" and "Implementing a Program to Use and Develop Intuition to Increase Productivity in Your Organization." Books, articles, audio-visual materials, and other resources are contained in each for your use and guidance.

NOTES

1. Weston H. Agor, *Intuitive Management: Integrating Left and Right Brain Management Skills* (Englewood Cliffs, NJ: Prentice-Hall, 1984).

2. The instrument used for the second part of this study is contained in the Appendix of this book. Based on what I learned through this field research, that open-ended questionnaire was substantially revised into a survey instrument for measuring intuitive ability, which is now available nationally. See Weston H. Agor, *Test Your Intuitive Power: AIM Survey* (Bryn Mawr, PA: Organization Design and Development, 1985).

Acknowledgments

I have to begin by reacknowledging all the same groups and individuals who helped me with my first book on this subject. Without their initial support and assistance, this book would not now be a reality.

To this manifest of "initial fellow travelers" should be added the staff and trustees of the Alden B. Dow Creativity Center in Midland, Michigan, which provided financial and staff support for conducting the field study that led to this book and for a 1984 Summer Residence Fellowship to carry out my research and field interviewing. Also thanks go to the University of Texas at El Paso, which provided a Presidential Mini-Grant and two Faculty Development Grants to attend seminars that helped me develop my own intuitive skills further and to collect materials for use on this topic in my graduate Masters in Public Administration program.

Appreciation also goes to Tom Smith, Jack Flynn, and Larry Saddler at the Dow Chemical Company in Midland, Michigan, who not only helped to arrange a number of personal interviews among top executives in their corporate head-quarters, but also helped refine my own thinking by constantly "testing" the direction in which I am headed. Special thanks also go to the private and public sector executives who either took the time to complete my rather long open-ended questionnaire or granted personal interviews so that I would have both the data base and the personal experience necessary to complete this study. I would also like to thank the many executives who have taken my workshops on the use and development of intuition. Preparing and delivering these workshops—and interacting with them—have helped me immensely to develop the daily exercises you will find in this book. The same can be said for my graduate students at the University of Texas at El Paso. The challenge of introducing them to a totally new concept and way of thinking taught me how to be more precise and straightforward in my own thinking. Special thanks to my typist, Florence Dick, who helped keep me on schedule and corrected the many errors

I made along the way. Thanks also to my editor, Tom Gannon, who believed in me and my work even before he joined this publisher.

Finally, thanks again to ''The Universal Mind,'' which has selected me to work on this project and guided me as far as I am today. It's been a fun trip!

The Logic of
Intuitive Decision
Making

PART I. The Logic of Intuitive Decision Making: A Research-Based Approach for Top Management

CHAPTER 1. The Logic for Using Intuition as a Brain Skill in Management

The decade of the 1980s may well become known as that benchmark period in management history when intuition finally gained acceptance as a powerful brain skill for guiding executive decision making. The first half of the decade has witnessed a crescendo of interest in the topic by both top executives and students of management alike, and certainly managers are far more comfortable today than was the case ten years ago to admit that they often actually use intuition to help make their most important decisions.[1]

For example, Thomas J. Peters and Robert H. Waterman, Jr., report in their best selling book, *In Search of Excellence*, that the ten best run companies in America now nurture the use and development of intuitive skills in their management cultures.[2] Similarly, John Naisbitt, the author of the classic book, *Megatrends*, points out in his newest book, *Reinventing the Corporation*, that using intuition in decision making has gained new respectability in corporate settings.[3] Well known scientists and inventors such as Jonas Salk and Buckminster Fuller have published books extolling the important role that intuition played in their most important discoveries,[4] and this subject has also received feature attention recently in such management magazines as the *Harvard Business Review*, *Organizational Dynamics*, and *Computer Decisions*.[5]

Why is there all of this interest in this brain skill right now? A number of reasons can easily be identified. One significant factor is that top managers often find that traditional analytical techniques (e.g., Management of Objectives [MBO], Program Evaluation Review Technique [PERT], forecasting) are not always as useful as they once were for guiding decisions (see Exhibit 1.1). This is so because top executives now have to make major decisions in a climate characterized by rapid change and at times also laden with crisis events. Frequently, totally new trends are emerging which make linear projection models based on past trends either inaccurate or misleading.[6] A classic case illustration is the $500 billion investment decision by major oil companies around the world

Exhibit 1.1
Brain Skills and Styles

Brain Skill Emphasized	Type of Organization Where Predominant	Task Preference	Problem Solving/Decision-Making Style	Example Applications	Sample Occupational Specialty
Thinking	Traditional Pyramid	Routine Precision Detail Implementation Repetitive	Deductive Objective Prefers solving problems by breaking down into parts, then approaching the problem sequentially using logic	Model building Projection	Planning Management Science Financial Management Engineering Law Enforcement Military
Intuitive	Open Temporary Rapidly changing	Non-routine Broad issues General policy options Constant new assignments	Inductive Subjective Prefers solving problems by looking at the whole then approaching the problem through hunches	Brainstorming Challenging traditional assumptions	Personnel Marketing Organization Development Intelligence

in 1980 and 1981. The straight line assumption that oil prices would continue to rise proved to "add up to one of the most expensive business errors ever," according to a study conducted by Arthur Andersen & Co., an accounting firm, and Cambridge Energy Research Associates, an energy consulting service.[7] They go on to argue that the oil industry is so turbulent "that future oil prices cannot be accurately predicted" using traditional methods.[8]

Another important reason why brain skills such as intuition are achieving increasing respectability in management circles is the progress made recently in brain research. The net product of recent research findings is that right brain processes and skills are being demystified and made more readily understandable and acceptable for general management use. For example, we understand better than ever today how different sections of the brain function, and we are learning more about how individual skills such as intuition emerge and can be cultivated for use in applied management settings.[9]

INTUITION AS A MANAGEMENT SKILL

Just what is intuition? Frances E. Vaughan, psychologist and author of the pioneering book *Awakening Intuition*, defines it as a "way of knowing . . . recognizing the possibilities in any situation."[10] *Webster's* defines intuition as "the power of knowing . . . a quick or ready apprehension."[11] Intuitive decisions come from a capacity to integrate information coming from both the left and the right sides of the brain. It is a product of both factual and feeling cues unclouded by deep personal ego involvement in the issue at hand.

It is perhaps best for us to think of intuition as being a *highly rational decision making skill*—one that is logical for managers to use.[12] For example, Laurence R. Sprecher, senior associate with Public Management Associates in Oregon, posits that intuition is really a *subspecies of logical thinking*—one in which the steps of the process are hidden in the subconscious portion of the brain. He argues that if we would accept the fact that intuition is an extension of the logical, we would be more comfortable using it.[13]

Put another way, just because modern science is not presently capable of explaining precisely step-by-step how intuition works does not mean that it is not a rational brain skill. It is important to remember that the history of science has been a constant process of redefining its perception of reality based on its ability to quantify what has always been true! For example, centuries ago, man was told by so-called hard science that if one ventured further than the eye could see, one would fall off the earth. Subsequently, science's increasing capacity to quantify led to a redefinition of "reality"—to that which has always been true. Similarly, in the field of brain research, new discoveries as to how the brain functions and can be more effectively used in the future are being made almost daily now. Hence, what might appear to be unexplainable to hard science today could well be perfectly understandable a decade from now.

LEVELS OF INTUITIVE AWARENESS

Intuitive cues come to executives on several different levels. Broadly speaking, intuition functions on four different levels: physical, emotional, mental, and spiritual.[14]

At the physical level, intuitive awareness comes in the form of bodily sensations. We have a strong body response to a person or situation when there is no apparent surface reason for having it. We simply know something without knowing how or why. Put another way, our intuition is telling us what our body already knows to be true.[15] At the emotional level, intuitive signals are transmitted in the form of feelings. For example, you might instantaneously sense that you like or dislike someone you just met without any readily apparent surface reason for doing so. Third, intuitive cues can come to you on a mental level. For example, you get a picture in your mind as to the direction to take after reviewing what appears to be a series of totally unrelated facts. Or, you find that you know what your business colleague is going to say before he/she says it. Finally, intuition can function on what is often called the spiritual level. Here, the executive has a good sense of how his/her acts are interlinked with the well being of all humanity. In business terms, this person understands that we now live in an interdependent world. An act taken in a corporate board room has repercussions that ultimately come back to impact the organization's own future. In this sense, no decision is taken in "private."

PRACTICAL USE OF INTUITION IN DECISION MAKING

Intuition, fully developed, is a highly efficient way of knowing. It is fast and accurate. Our system will process a wide array of information on many levels and give us an instantaneous cue, how to act. We have the answer even though we do not understand all the steps or know fully all the information our system processed to give us this cue. The more open we are to our feelings, the more secure we become through practice in their ability to give us correct cues; and the less we project our own personal desires and wishes for particular situations or persons to be other than they really are, the more efficient our intuitive clues will become.[16]

As a practical management tool for decision making, what does this mean? It means that through practice we can learn to use our intuition to help make decisions successfully and reduce unnecessary delay in the process. For example, frequently at work, we have an intuitive understanding of a person or situation. But, normally we are afraid to act on the basis of this instant awareness of our feelings. Instead, we tend to fall back on the tape we have often been socialized to program: "You had better wait, gather more facts, get to know the person or situation better." So, we often delay unnecessarily our actions and our decisions. What we do then is push our immediate feel for the situation or person into our subconscious for a while. Until we feel comfortable enough through actual day-to-day life experience to allow our feelings to surface again to our conscious mind (e.g., we work with a person for six months), we do not come to fully understand why we felt the way we did months before when we failed to act on our instantaneous feelings.

Many leading executives across the country have learned to use and rely on their intuition to help make decisions successfully. Regular work and practice with this brain skill have enabled these executives to find the way intuition functions most effectively for them. Carl Jung, the famous psychologist, found in his research that managers who become skilled in the use of their intuition tend to possess particular decision-making skills not normally possessed by others. They

- see new possibilities in any given situation;
- have a sense or vision of what is coming in the future and how to move their organization in response to it;
- are adept at generating new ideas and in providing ingenious new solutions to old problems;
- deal effectively with rapid change, crisis, and highly complex decision-making situations.[17]

These are skills that would appear increasingly useful in the "megatrend" management environment we are now entering. For example, many of the products that companies will need to depend on in the future do not even exist today. The capacity to "dream up" these new products will become a premium skill. Similarly, the capacity to make sense out of the array of facts all around you and pick out the new emerging trends that should shape your future course of action will also become a premium skill in this environment.

FIELD TESTING FOR INTUITIVE DECISION-MAKING SKILLS

It is a reasonably safe bet then that intuition as a decision making skill will grow in importance in the decade ahead. This probability is the reason why I began a series of major field studies starting in 1981 concerning executives' ability to use intuition—and their actual use of this brain skill—to make management decisions.

Over 3,000 managers across the country have now been tested in a wide variety of organizational settings (business, government, education, military, and health), at all levels of management responsibility, and in various occupational specializations. My goal was to find out just how intuitive actual managers appeared to be, and to determine if there was any significant variation from organization to organization and by management level. I also was interested in determining whether intuitive ability varied by sex, by ethnic background, and by occupational specialty. Finally, I wished to determine how those executives who scored high in intuitive ability actually used their brain skill to help make management decisions. The answers to these questions appeared to hold important information that could be used practically by individuals and organizations to increase productivity and overall job satisfaction in a variety of specific ways (e.g., how to design or redesign some of our present personnel and organizational development programs).

The groups tested included a wide horizontal range of different organizations and settings including private sector chief executive officers (CEOs), emergency preparedness military personnel, community college presidents, state health and rehabilitative services managers, city managers, state legislators and staff, professional civil servants, and executives who have taken my workshops across the country. Responses were stratified for such key variables as level of management, level of government, sex, occupational specialization, and ethnic background. All the responses were analyzed by computer, and all the findings were subject to statistical significance tests (see Chapter 2 for further details).

TEST INSTRUMENTS USED

Over the series of field studies, two instruments were used. The instrument used to measure underlying intuitive ability consisted of twelve questions selected from the Myers–Briggs Type Indicator (MBTI), a psychological instrument that, among other things, measures your ability to use intuition, as contrasted from thinking ability, to make decisions.[18] This instrument was selected for use because it has been widely applied in practical settings across the country, and has been proven to have a high degree of reliability and validity as a test instrument.[19] A scale was constructed for this part of the test so that each manager could be ranked exactly from top to bottom on how he/she scored individually, and also how he/she compared to other managers taking the test. The maximum score was 12 (highly intuitive) with a minimum score of 0 (little or no intuitive ability presently apparent).

The second instrument measures whether the manager tested actually uses his/her intuitive ability to make important decisions, and if so, how. These questions were designed for follow-up testing based on the pattern of responses received after administering the first instrument.[20] Those executives who scored in the top 10 percent nationally on their ability to use their intuition to make management decisions were tested to see if and how they actually used their skill to help make decisions. The instrument was also designed to obtain data on a number of related questions such as whether executives who used intuition to guide their decisions actually shared this fact openly with their colleagues or kept it a secret instead (see Exhibit 1.2).

When taken together, these two instruments become a powerful tool for measuring a manager's (or total organization's) intuitive decision making style and ability.[21] Turn now to Chapters 2 and 3 to find the dramatic results from this extensive field testing.

Exhibit 1.2
Intuitive Management Survey

PART	PURPOSE	STYLE POSSIBLE
I (12 questions from MBTI)	Measures under-lying potential ability	Intuitive (I) Thinking (T)
II (10 questions self-designed)	Measures actual use of ability in decision making	Use (U) Not use (NU) Open (O) Closed (C)
TOTAL AIM Survey (Agor Intuitive Management)	Measures both potential and actual use	I-U, O I-U, C I-NU, C

NOTES

1. Ten years ago, it is unlikely that the study reported here could have been conducted. In 1974 Douglas Dean and his colleagues found that executives were extremely reluctant to admit that they actually used intuition to make major business decisions. Only after "objective measurement" of their ability was presented to them did they reveal their skills in this area. For details, see Douglas Dean and John Mihalasky, *Executive ESP* (Englewood Cliffs, NJ: Prentice-Hall, 1974). Since that time, executives have become more open about discussing their intuitive ability, and articles in major "main line" publications are now becoming commonplace. For example, see Louis R. Pondy, "Union of Rationality and Intuition in Management Action," in Suresh Sirvastra and Associates, eds., *The Executive Mind: New Insights on Managerial Thought and Action* (San Francisco: Jossey-Bass, 1983), pp. 169–91.

2. Thomas J. Peters and Robert H. Waterman, Jr., *In Search of Excellence: Lessons from America's Best-Run Companies* (New York: Harper & Row, 1982), pp. 60–62.

3. John Naisbitt, *Megatrends: Ten New Directions Transfroming Our Lives* (New

York: Warner Books, 1984); John Naisbitt and Patricia Aburdene, *Reinventing the Corporation* (New York: Warner Books, 1985).

4. Jonas Salk, *Anatomy of Reality: Merging of Intuition and Reason* (New York: Columbia University Press, 1983); R. Buckminster Fuller, *Intuition* (San Luis Obispo, CA: Impact Publishers, 1983).

5. Daniel J. Isenberg, "How Senior Managers Think," *Harvard Business Review* (November–December 1984), pp. 81–90; Weston H. Agor, "The Logic of Intuition: How Successful Executives Make Important Decisions," *Organizational Dynamics* (Winter 1986), pp. 5–18; Martin Lasden, "Intuition: The Voice of Success?" *Computer Decisions* (February 26, 1985), pp. 98–104.

6. See, e.g., Laurie McGinley, "Forecasters Overhaul 'Models' of Economy in Wake of 1982 Errors," *Wall Street Journal* (February 17, 1983), pp. 1 and 20.

7. "Researchers Call Oil Investments Expensive Errors," Associated Press News Wire, December 4, 1984.

8. Ibid.

9. See, e.g., Floyd R. Bloom, Laura Hofstadter, and Arlyne Lazerson, *Textbook: Brain, Mind, and Behavior* (New York: W. H. Freeman & Co., 1984). Particularly intriguing is the research by Richard Bergland of Harvard University who has developed the concept of the brain as a gland, which controls the secretion of several hundred chemicals that affect our thinking skills. See Norman Cousins, "An Adventure of Ideas," *New Realities* 5, 1 (1983), pp. 11–12.

10. Frances E. Vaughan, *Awakening Intuition* (Garden City, NY: Anchor Books, 1979).

11. *Webster's New World Dictionary* (Cleveland, OH: William Collins Publishers, 1980).

12. For a discussion of research on how the mind works in this regard, see D. N. Perkins, *The Mind's Best Work* (Cambridge, MA: Harvard University Press, 1981).

13. "Intuition, Anyone?" *Public Management* (February 1983), p. 18.

14. This treatment on levels of intuitive awareness is discussed in Vaughan, *Awakening Intuition*, pp. 66–80.

15. Recent research indicates that we can be influenced by extrasensory stimulus even when we are not aware of it at the conscious level. See, e.g., Tony Bastick, *Intuition: How We Think and Act* (New York: John Wiley & Sons, 1982).

16. For a detailed discussion of how this process works, see Frances E. Vaughan's cassette tape, "Exercises for Awakening the Intuitive You" (Washington, DC: American Psychological Association, 1982).

17. Isabel Briggs Myers, *Introduction to Type* (Palo Alto, CA: Consulting Psychologists Press, 1980). For more recent findings, see Gordon Lawrence, *People Types and Tiger Stripes: A Practical Guide to Learning Styles*, 2nd ed. (Gainesville, FL: Center for Applications of Psychological Type, 1982) and Malcolm R. Westcott, *Toward a Contemporary Psychology of Intuition: A Historical, Theoretical, and Empirical Enquiry* (New York: Holt, Rinehart, Winston, 1968).

18. You will note that for the purposes of this test, I have used the term *thinking* as opposed to *sensing*, which is the term used in the MBTI. The reason is that during my pretesting I found that *thinking* was clearer to managers than the term *sensing* to depict analytical and deductive processes. Since I was not using the other dimensions of the MBTI here, it did not cause confusion to make this change in terms.

19. For details on the MBTI, see Isabel Briggs Myers, *The Myers–Briggs Type In-*

dicator:1985 Manual (Palo Alto, CA: Consulting Psychologists Press, 1985). Also see the publications and research on the MBTI instrument published by the Center for Applications of Psychological Type in Gainesville, Florida.

20. For details see Weston H. Agor, *AIM Survey: Trainer Guide* (Bryn Mawr, PA: Organization Design and Development, 1985).

21. For details see Weston H. Agor, *Test Your Intuitive Powers: AIM Survey* (Bryn Mawr, PA: Organization Design and Development, 1985).

CHAPTER 2. The Intuitive Ability of Executives: Findings from Field Research

Several criteria were used to select the managers to be tested nationally. First, an effort was made to select managers from a wide horizontal range of different organizations and settings. This was done so that whatever the findings turned out to be, statements could be made more precisely about conditions under which the results appeared or did not appear to be valid in organizational life (e.g., for only certain organizations and settings vs. all). Second, in each of the groups selected, an effort was made to obtain a representative sample of the total management structure so that meaningful statements (statistically significant) could be made from the findings about what the intuitive management style and ability were really like in each organization. Third, access also played a part in the organizations actually selected. In each management group tested, a major peer leader or top manager provided the necessary access to ensure that the questionnaire instrument was distributed and returned at a high rate.

For the first stage of my study, which involved the measurement of intuitive ability, more than 6,500 questionnaires were distributed between 1981 and 1985. From this group, actual responses received totaled 3,100 (46 percent). The response rate for all the groups tested was so high because peer leaders either wrote cover letters explaining the test instrument and encouraged each manager to return the questionnaire or they provided direct access to the management groups tested. Exhibit 2.1 summarizes that range of management groups actually tested along with response rates. For the private sector, eighty-eight CEOs were included as well as management groups from such major organizations as Dow Chemical Company, Walt Disney Enterprises, Tenneco Oil, and several of the companies in the Bell telephone system. For the public sector, a large random sample of the public administration profession was included (membership of the American Society for Public Administration [ASPA] minus academics), three large sample groups representing three of the largest states in the nation (California, Florida, and Michigan), and samples from workshop groups tested at the

Exhibit 2.1
Range of Groups Sampled

GROUP	NUMBER SAMPLED	RESPONSE RATE NUMBER	(%)
Private Sector			
• South Florida CEOs of major corporations	88	54	(61)
• Managers from other sample sets	734	734	(100)
TOTAL	822	788	(96)
Public Sector			
• National survey sample of ASPA members	5,000	1,679	(34)
• Three State Sample			
• Civil servants	285	261	(92)
• Educators	100	43	(43)
• Military	50	44	(88)
• Politicians	110	47	(44)
• City managers	157	63	(40)
SUBTOTAL	702	458	(65)
• Managers from Workshops	175	458	(100)
Total Private and Public Sector Samples	6,699	3,100	(46)

Federal Executive Institute, the National Security Agency, and the City of Phoenix.[1]

The second stage of my study, which was completed in 1984–85, involved the actual use of intuitive ability. For this stage of my study, I selected as my sample group for follow-up study only those executives who scored in the top 10 percent on the intuition scale from the national sample population previously tested. The reasoning for selecting this group was that if intuition were actually being used as a decision making skill, it should be most apparent to and among those executives who had the highest ability to use it. One hundred top executives have been tested in depth here, including major executives at the corporate headquarters of General Motors and Dow Chemical Company and board members of such major organizations as Chrysler, Burroughs, and the Ford Foundation.

Responses were stratified by such key variables as level of management, level of government, sex, occupational specialization, and ethnic background. All the responses were analyzed by computer, and all the findings were subject to statistical significance tests. That is, are the differences found in scale scores between management levels, sex, occupational specialty, and ethnic background likely to occur by chance—or are they a measure of the actual differences that exist between these groups?[2]

TEST FINDINGS

The findings from this national testing are dramatic!* Clearly, intuitive management ability appears to vary by management level, by level of government service, by sex, by occupational specialty, and, to some degree, by ethnic background.[3]

Top Managers

Intuition appears to be a skill that is more prevalent as one moves up the management ladder. Top managers in every sample group tested scored higher than middle/lower level managers in their underlying ability to use intuition to make decisions (see Exhibit 2.2). It also appears that the higher one goes in the level of government service (from county to national), the greater the ability to use intuition becomes (see Exhibit 2.3). As outlined in Chapter 1, it appears plausible that one of the skills that top managers rely on most frequently is their intuitive ability to make the right decisions.

For example, as Donald A. Schon points out in a recent book entitled *The Reflective Practitioner: How Professionals Think in Action*, they have had to constantly make choices in turbulent environments where problems do not lend

*From *Intuitive Management: Integrated Left and Right Brain Management Skills*. By Weston H. Agor © Weston H. Agor. Reprinted by permission of the publisher, Prentice-Hall, Inc., Englewood Cliffs, N.J.

Exhibit 2.2
Score on Intuition Scale by Level of Management

Intuition Scale	Group Sampled			
	Private Sector		Public Sector	
	Level of Management		Level of Management	
	Top	Middle/ Lower	Top	Middle/ Lower
Maximum Score (12)				
High (8-12)				
	6.5			
			6.2	
Average (4-6)		5.8		5.6
Low (1-3)				
No Score				

Exhibit 2.3
Score on Intuition Scale by Level of Government

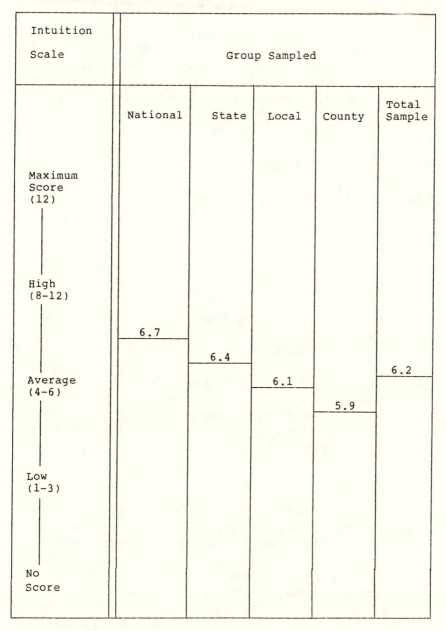

Intuition Scale	Group Sampled				
	National	State	Local	County	Total Sample
Maximum Score (12)					
High (8-12)					
	6.7				
		6.4			
					6.2
Average (4-6)			6.1		
				5.9	
Low (1-3)					
No Score					

themselves to the techniques of benefit–cost analysis or to probabilistic reasoning.[4] Similarly, Martin Lasden in a recent article in *Computer Decisions* reports that top executives he interviewed in the computer industry assert time and again that intuition is a critical factor in their success at making the right decision.[5]

When executives in top management positions who also score in the top 10 percent in intuitive ability are tested, the results overwhelmingly indicate that these executives do use their brain skill to guide their most important decisions. Not only do the vast majority of these top executives admit that they use intuition to help guide their most important decisions, but they go on to specify the situations and settings in which they find their intuition is *most helpful* in making key management decisions:

• There is a high level of uncertainty.
• There is little previous precedent.
• Variables are often not scientifically predictable.
• "Facts" are limited.
• Facts do not clearly point the way to go.
• Time is limited and there is pressure to be right.
• There are several plausible alternative solutions to choose from, with good arguments for each.

It is also significant to note that when these top managers intuitively "know" they have reached the correct decision, they share a "consensus set" of feelings that tell them so: a sense of excitement—almost euphoria; a total sense of commitment; a feeling of total harmony; warmth and confidence; a burst of enthusiasm and energy like a bolt of lightning or sudden flash that "this is the solution." Alternatively, when they sense an impending decision may be an incorrect one or that they need to take more time to adequately process the cues they are receiving, these managers speak of feelings of anxiety, mixed signals, discomfort, or an upset stomach.[6]

Sex Differences

Another extremely important finding is that there are statistically significant differences between the sexes regarding intuitive ability for both private and public sector executives. Women consistently scored higher on the intuition scale than men in every group sampled (see Exhibit 2.4). This fact is supported by other research that has recently appeared. For example, one group of research findings suggests that there may be different patterns of physiological growth of the brain for men and women, which could help to account for some of the score difference.[7] Another possible explanation is that women have learned culturally to use and develop their native intuitive ability. In contrast, men historically

Exhibit 2.4
Score on Intuition Scale by Sex

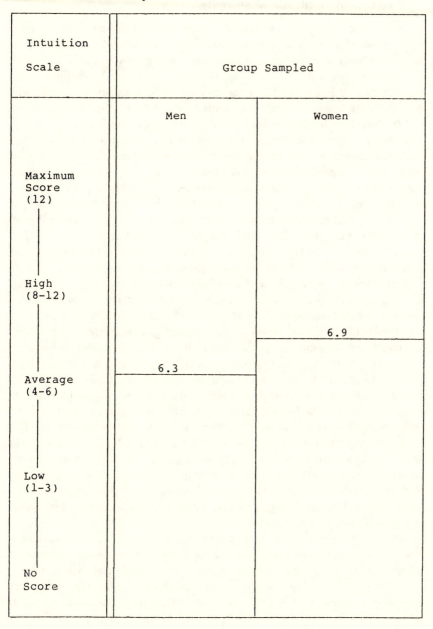

have learned through societal and cultural pressure to suppress feelings and to rely on deductive processes vs. inductive ones.[8]

Differences by Occupational Specialty

It would not be surprising to find differences in intuitive scores for managers by occupational specialty in organizations across the country. Historically, certain professions such as engineering, financial management, and law enforcement, e.g., have emphasized analytical, quantitative, and deductive techniques for decision making in preference to management skills normally associated with the use of intuition. Presumably, executives would also self-select themselves to that profession that emphasized the brain skills they excelled in.[9]

At the same time, one might expect that as one moved from lower/middle levels of management to top management in any professional specialty, the skills required for successful decision making would change in character. Top management positions would appear to be more likely to require a greater capacity to solve complex problems, deal with uncertainty, motivate subordinates to act, and integrate factual information along with personal needs, wants, and preferences into an effective management program that could be implemented. This job description would seem to place a greater premium on the ability to use intuitive brain skills to help guide management choices.[10]

Available test scores indicate that intuitive ability does vary significantly by occupational specialization and by management level within occupations. Take, e.g., the occupational specializations of general administration and policy as compared with the specializations of financial management and law enforcement. We might expect managers specializing in financial management and law enforcement to have higher test scores on thinking vs. intuitive ability since these professions tend to place greater emphasis on facts and figures for decision making, value hierarchical models of management, and stress quantitative techniques of analysis. On the other hand, we would probably expect that the brain skill used most in the other two occupational specialties might be intuition. This is so because general administration and policy tend to be broader in scope. The issues a manager would be more likely to face would probably be significantly more complex. Elements of uncertainty and rapid change might be more common problems that would have to be dealt with along with a complex array of clientele groups demanding conflicting services. Intuitive skills in this context would appear to be particularly useful.

Exhibit 2.5 compares the intuitive scale scores by occupational specialties. You will note that managers in general administration and policy clearly have higher intuition scores than managers specializing in financial management or law enforcement. However, as we move up the management ladder within each occupational specialty, it is important to note that top managers tend to score higher in intuitive ability across the board (see Exhibit 2.6).

Now this does not suggest that top managers in these occupations necessarily

Exhibit 2.5
Score on Intuition Scale by Occupational Specialty

Intuition Scale	Thinking ◄─── Range of ───► Intuitive Scores				
	Financial Management/Law Enforcement	Military	Health	General Administration /Policy	Personnel
Maximum Score (12)					
High (8-12)					7.9
				6.7	
Average (4-6)			6.3		
		5.1			
	4.9				
Low (1-3)					
No Score					

Exhibit 2.6
Score on Intuition Scale Within Occupational Specialty by Management Level

Selected Occupational Specialties	Level of Management		
	Top	Middle/Lower	Total
General Administration/ Policy	6.9	6.4	6.6
Health	6.8	6.5	6.5
Financial Management	6.1	5.7	5.9
Engineering	6.0	5.6	5.8
Law Enforcement	6.5	5.9	6.0
TOTAL	6.5	5.8	6.4

have an inherently higher intuitive ability at the outset than middle/lower level managers. This may indeed be true in part. But as we shall see in Chapter 3, my field research suggests it is also probably due to the fact that these top managers have learned through practice to develop their inherent ability to the point that they can use this brain skill effectively on-the-job to make decisions. In fact, it could well be that managers aspiring to top levels of responsibility in their respective organizations need to learn to make this transition before their career goals can be successfully achieved.

Ethnic Background

Managers tested were also asked to identify their ethnic background. The purpose was to determine if there were any discernible differences in intuitive ability. Since the vast majority of the respondents classified themselves as white, only two other groups (Asians and blacks) had large enough numbers represented to statistically measure whether significant differences were apparent.

The available data indicate that managers from Asian ethnic backgrounds appear to have a higher level of intuitive ability than the average manager who responded (see Exhibit 2.7). As has been suggested by Richard Pascale and Anthony Athos in *The Art of Japanese Management*, this could well mean that managers who were brought up in Asian family background settings were socialized from birth to emphasize and practice the Eastern world's approach to life, which encourages the development of intuitive brain skills.[11] One of the practical implications of these findings is that executives with Asian ethnic

Exhibit 2.7
Score on Intuition Scale by Ethnic Background

Intuition Scale	Thinking ◄——— Range of ———► Intuitive Scores		
	Black	White	Asian
Maximum Score (12)			
High (8-12)			
			6.5
		6.2	
Average (4-6)			
	5.2		
Low (1-3)			
No Score			

backgrounds could potentially be highly effective in management settings where intuitive skills are a premium (e.g., crisis management, brainstorming).

Black managers, on the other hand, appeared to score somewhat lower than the mean respondent on intuitive ability. Taken at face value, it would appear that black managers, on the average at present, would function best in situations where thinking vs. intuitive brain skills are emphasized. Examples would be management situations where authority patterns are clear and where the management task requires detail precision. Black managers aspiring to top management positions or occupational specialties requiring an emphasis on intuitive brain skills could also probably benefit from workshop and training programs that would develop their ability to use these skills more effectively than they presently appear able to do.

Job Satisfaction

One of the questions that was asked managers was whether they liked their present position or occupation. Nearly 6 percent of the respondents indicated that they did not. When their scores on the intuition test were examined alongside the occupations in which they were specializing, the findings were striking. The common thread throughout the data appeared to be that the vast majority of these managers had selected an occupational specialization that did not comfortably match their brain style preferences. These findings suggest that there is considerable opportunity within organizations for increasing not only job satisfaction but also productivity if these individuals could be more appropriately placed where their brain skills fit more comfortably.

SUMMARY

So far, we have reported on how the intuitive ability of managers varies in the national sample group tested. One of the most significant findings is that top managers on average score higher than their subordinates in every sample group tested. We have also found that women score higher than men on average, that there are significant differences by occupational specialty, and that Asian managers score the highest among all ethnic groups for which data are available. Chapter 3 will now outline in detail how these highly intuitive executives (those who score in the top 10 percent nationally) actually use this brain skill to guide their most important decisions.

NOTES

1. Private sector CEOs were made up of a sample of 88 top executives who were members of the Greater Miami Chamber of Commerce in Florida. Ray Goode, president of the Babcock Company in Coral Gables, Florida, and former Dade County manager, wrote a cover letter endorsing the questionnaire and mailed the test out of his office over

his letterhead. Other private sector executives tested were from a wide variety of sample groups. Access to some groups was gained through the Alden B. Dow Creativity Center in Midland, Michigan, which helped support some of my research on this study. Other samples came from executives who had taken my workshops across the country for such organizations as Tenneco Oil, several Bell system companies, and Walt Disney Enterprises.

Public sector samples were gathered as follows. All the community college presidents in California were mailed the test over Dan Angel's signature, then president of Citrus Community College in Azusa, California, and former state legislator in Michigan. Neil E. Allgood, brigadier general and director of the California Specialized Training Institute in San Luis Obispo, California, administered the test personally to his 40th Infantry Division emergency management staff. David Pingree, secretary of the Florida State Department of Health and Rehabilitative Services in Tallahassee, Florida, mailed the test out of his office with a cover letter of support to 110 of his managers statewide. Robert Donly, president of the Florida League of Cities in 1982, also wrote a cover letter explaining the test that was mailed to city managers in Florida statewide. State legislators and staff were tested in Michigan with the assistance of Senator Robert Vander Laan, former State Senate majority leader, whom I served as executive assistant in 1973–74. In addition, the ASPA meeting attendees of Orange and Los Angeles counties were tested in the spring of 1982. Together, nearly 800 executives were mailed questionnaires besides the national random sample of the ASPA profession. The national ASPA mailing was endorsed with a joint cover letter by three national council members at the time—Gus Turnbull III (who was also a member of the board of editors of *Public Administration Review*), Jerry O'Neil, and Carolyn B. Lawrence.

Finally, the public sector sample was completed with executives who had taken my workshops across the country, representing such organizations as the National Security Agency, the Federal Executive Institute, and the City of Phoenix.

2. The statistical test, one-way analysis of variance, was used to measure significance. The standard of 0.05 or better was established for rejecting the null hypothesis; i.e., the chances of obtaining the differences in scores noted was five times in one hundred or less. For a discussion of how this procedure is conducted, see Lyman Ott and David K. Hildebrand, *Statistical Thinking for Managers* (Boston: Duxbury Press, 1983).

3. For a much more detailed discussion of the findings reported in this chapter, see Weston H. Agor, *Intuitive Management Integrating Left and Right Brain Management Skills* (Englewood Cliffs, NJ: Prentice-Hall, 1984).

4. Donald A. Schon, *The Reflective Practitioner—How Professionals Think in Action* (New York: Basic Books, 1983).

5. Martin Lasden, "Intuition: The Voice of Success?" *Computer Decisions* (February 26, 1985), p. 98.

6. See Chapter 3 for more details on how top managers use their intuitive ability to make important decisions.

7. Pamela Weintraub, "The Brain: His and Hers," *Discover* (April 1981), pp. 15–20.

8. Alice G. Sargent, *The Androgynous Manager* (New York: AMACOM, 1981). It should also be noted that recent brain research at UCLA conducted by Eran Zaidel also suggests that women possess a better corpus callosum, the hard, fibrous band in the center of the brain that bridges the two hemispheres. This helps enable women to better switch information from one side of the brain to the other—hence a capacity to integrate intuitive

cues into applied settings. Zaidel also notes the right hemisphere of the brain is especially important in processing new information and in putting things together from individual parts, which is one intuitive process.

9. Available research thus far does seem to indicate that personality types vary significantly by occupational specialization. See Isabel Briggs Myers and Peter B. Myers, *Gifts Differing* (Palo Alto, CA: Consulting Psychologists Press, 1980), particularly Chapter 14 on occupations and types.

10. For a discussion of this possibility, see Al Siebert, "The Survivor Personality," *Portland Oregonian–Northwest Magazine* (January 27, 1980).

11. Richard Tanner Pascale and Anthony G. Athos, *The Art of Japanese Management: Applications for American Executives* (New York: Warner Books, 1981), especially Chapter 4 on Zen and the art of management.

CHAPTER 3. How Top Executives Use Intuition to Make Decisions: Findings from Field Research

Thus far we have discussed the test results on executives' ability to use intuition to guide management decisions. Now let us see whether the executives who score in the top 10 percent nationally in this brain skill (10 to 12 range on the intuition scale) actually use this ability to help make important decisions, and if so, in what way.

As noted in Chapter 2, I prepared a special list of questions to test those executives who scored in this top range on the intuition scale. I asked a battery of questions to enable me to probe deeply into how managers actually use their intuitive ability to help guide their subsequent decisions.[1] I had two major goals. The first was to obtain a *more complete picture* of how the total intuitive decision making process works than research data presently provide. Second, these findings, it was hoped, would give me a *sound research-based foundation* upon which training programs could be developed. Managers then could be more productively guided as to how to use and further develop their inherent intuitive ability for day-to-day use in decision making.

RESEARCH FINDINGS

One hundred detailed survey responses were obtained. As a whole, this set of data gives us a much better picture than we have ever had of how highly intuitive executives actually use their ability to help make critical decisions. These research findings also reveal a number of practical tools and techniques that can be used by other executives to help them develop their own intuitive ability more effectively.

Actual Use of Intuition to Guide Decisions

When asked the question, "Do you believe you use intuition to guide your most important decisions?", all but one of the top executives responding said that they do. One experienced executive describes the process this way: "I don't think intuition is some magical thing. I think it is a subconscious drawing from innumerable experiences which are stored. You draw from this reserve without conscious thought."[2] Another respondent volunteers:

I do believe in using my intuitive powers on most of my decisions be they large or small. This is not a conscious effort on my behalf. After a lifetime of dealing with people and people problems and with many of these dealings having a real life or death outcome, I feel that most life experiences are similar, and when they happen they are objective and pragmatic. These I store in the recesses of my mind for recall at later times when decisions must be made.[3]

These executives' descriptions of how the intuitive process works for them are much like that outlined by Frances E. Vaughan, psychologist and author of *Awakening Intuition*, which is probably the best book on this topic generally available today. She states:

At any given moment one is conscious of only a small portion of what one knows. Intuition allows one to draw on that vast storehouse of unconscious knowledge that includes not only everything that one has experienced or learned, either consciously or subliminally, but also the infinite reservoir of the collective or universal unconscious, in which individual separateness and ego boundaries are transcended.[4]

As a group, however, these top executives are quick to point out that they consider intuition to be only one resource for guiding their decisions. They are not advocating that intuition be relied upon exclusively or that more traditional management practices be abandoned. On the other hand, respondents do recognize that intuition itself is a key management resource that should not be ignored or abandoned either. Many top executives also stress that they believe that good intuitive decisions are in part based on input from facts and experience gained over the years combined and integrated with a well honed sensitivity/openness to other more right brain cues. This advice is well summed up by William G. McGinnis, city manager of Crescent City, California, who offers this rather humorous but also rather wise operating definition of an intuitive decision: "I believe that good intuitive decisions are directly proportional to one's years of challenging experience, plus the number of related and worthwhile years of training and education, all divided by lack of confidence or the fear of being replaced."[5]

When Intuition Is Most Useful

Clearly, respondents find that their intuitive ability is particularly useful to them when faced with management situations that are characteristic of the megatrend environment we are now entering. When executives are asked, "When using your intuition, have you found it functions best only with *certain* problems/ issues/circumstances or do you use it freely to help guide *all* your major decisions?", they identify these situations and circumstances where they find this brain skill serves them best:

- where there is a high level of uncertainty;
- where there is little previous precedent;
- where variables are less scientifically predictable;
- where "facts" are limited;
- where facts do not clearly indicate the direction to take;
- when analytical data are of little use (e.g., new trends are emerging);
- where there are several plausible alternative solutions to choose from, with good arguments for each;
- where time is limited and there is pressure to be right;
- for negotiations and personnel decisions.

We can all think of typical management decisions when one or several of these conditions prevail. For example, if you were buying women's fashions for next year, could you rely on data projected from last year's fashion styles? Or, whatever the pattern of data for the last five years concerning oil prices, could you rely on these figures alone to project what the future oil prices are likely to be? The answer in both cases is obviously not. These are circumstances and settings that top executives must contend with as "standard fare" as they attempt to make the right decision.

When respondents themselves are asked about whether in such decision making situations they "can give . . . an example or two of a very important decision where you followed your intuition and it proved to be the right one," *every one* of these highly intuitive executives did so, and in detail. Exhibit 3.1 summarizes some of the more representative examples given by both private and public sector executives. You will note that these decisions are indeed of strategic magnitude— often involving many millions of dollars, affecting the public welfare, and even setting the course for the organization in question for years to come. When viewed as a whole, all of the decisions that top executives recall do indeed fall into management situations that they identify as most conducive to intuitive decision making: They involve a high degree of risk; require a choice between several plausible options, none of which is clearly favored by the data available; or involve making a decision where data may be inadequate or where the course chosen is even in conflict with the direction suggested by the data at hand.

Here are samples of how these executives recall some of their most important intuitive decisions. One highly placed respondent identifies recommending that the company he works for (one of the largest chemical conglomerates in the country) not invest in a $500 million capital project. His "feel for the future" proved to be correct, and the company has had to take a substantial loss as a result of discounting his advice.

Exhibit 3.1

Representative Examples of Strategic Decisions Guided by Intuition

---

- Recommended not to invest in a $500 million capital project which was supported by our scientific staff, that we were technically capable of implementing but that I questioned economically.

- Refused to pull a drug off the market as recommended by the FDA based on adverse animal reactions to tests.

- Decided a multi-million dollar production expansion at one of our major plants with a strong quality performance record in favor of another plant with lower production costs but a poorer quality performance record.

- Supported the regional decentralization of the mental health department statewide over strong internal objections.

- Moved my troops the morning after dreaming our location would be hit by a shell attack which in fact happened shortly later.

I recommended that we not invest in a 500 million dollar capital project which later was a technical success but an economic failure. The investment will be a total loss for us or, at best, be sold for 25% of its original value. My own recommendation was a judgment call requiring intuitive feel for future events.[6]

At times, taking the risk of following one's own intuitive cues in the face of "facts" that point in another direction can signify putting your very career on the line. One executive remembers well his intuitive decision for this very reason: "I refused to agree with the Federal Drug Administration to pull a drug off the market based on an adverse animal reaction. I nearly killed myself in the short run in the organization on that one."[7] However, events which unfolded later proved that his intuitive call was the right one, and he survived unscathed.

This little story that one respondent tells is a good example of an executive following his intuition when no other "factual" evidence pointed in that direction:

Shortly after assuming office, there was a young man working in the department who had a lovely wife and young child. They were a devoted and close family, and from all surface appearances, it looked like he would be a trusted employee. Within a short time, things just didn't seem quite right. I could not identify the cause of my uneasiness because he seemed conscientious in every way. On a hunch, I called the sheriff and said, "Don't ask me why I'm asking you to do me this favor, but I'd like you to check on this employee. He's a good worker, but certain things are just not adding up. Will you please investigate him for me and call me back." The sheriff called back that afternoon and said, "You're about to lose a good employee. He's wanted in North Carolina." Here again my intuition served me well.[8]

If we accept executive self-evaluations that the "intuition guided decisions" named were in fact successful ones, the question remains, How do respondents know which course to take when they are faced with the choices they have in front of them? These intuitive executives describe in common the feelings they experience at the point of decision: "a sense of excitement—almost euphoric"; "growing excitement in the pit of my stomach"; "a total sense of commitment"; "a feeling of total harmony"; "warm, confident"; "a burst of enthusiasm, energy"; "it feels like a bolt of lightning or sudden flash that this is the solution."

A former state governor who is now a member of the corporate boards of Chrysler and Burroughs as well as the Ford Foundation recalls how he felt when he made the critical decision in 1976 to put state troopers on the highways in Detroit to control crime:

I made the decision quickly without all the facts, or what the costs would be to carry the decision out. When it's a critical decision like this and it has to be made quickly—even if the issue arose only moments ago—something clicks, and I say "let's go!"[9]

Another respondent describes a very similar feeling when he knows his intuitive decision is the right one to take: "Like the beer commercial, 'when it's right you know it.' There appears to be a 'certainness' of the decision—an undeniable rightness which feels very comfortable."[10]

Alternatively, these executives also seem to share a common set of feeling experiences when they sense an impending decision may be an incorrect one, that a particular option is inappropriate, or that they need to take more time to adequately process the cues they are receiving in order to arrive at the best decision possible. At these times, managers speak of feeling "a sense of anxiety," "mixed signals being received," "discomfort," "sleepless nights," or an "upset stomach." The president of one of the most successful companies in the United States uses these cues as a basis for taking action:

We call them 3 A.M. decisions around here. You wake up in the middle of the night with the decision as to what to do or not do. I often use my intuition to delay a decision or to wait for more new information to come in. Knowing when to procrastinate is a key skill.[11]

It is important to note that the intuitive cues these top executives just identified as helpful guides for making key decisions are similar to those described by other successful executives and artists interviewed by other researchers. For example, Marilee Zdenek interviewed many famous personalities ranging across widely different fields for her recent book, *The Right-Brain Experience*. She found that these persons are clearly aware that they use intuition to guide their most important decisions, and receive cues similar to those mentioned above.

One of the most intriguing interviews she relates is with I. B. Melchior, a former counter-espionage agent and present agent/writer. Melchior actively used his intuition to survive in a number of dangerous and uncertain situations during World War II when he was working in counter-intelligence. The skill that he developed then continues to serve him well in his present occupational roles.[12]

Factors That Impede the Use of Intuition

It appears then that intuitive executives receive clear signals that act as guideposts—telling them when they have chosen a workable option, when they have not, and when they need to take more time before reaching a final decision. But, if this is indeed the case, why are these executives not always correct, then? For cues, executives were also asked, "Can you give me an example or two of a very important decision where you followed your intuition and it proved to be the *wrong* one?" If they had a response to this question, I also then asked, "Thinking back now about these times, can you pinpoint any specific factors about yourself or your surroundings which seemed to exist or be present when your decision appeared to be wrong?"

What emerges from executive responses suggests that they indeed make errors in their decisions. But these errors do not appear to be caused by following their intuition. Rather, *faulty decisions appear instead to be caused by failing to follow their intuition*. That is, when these top executives make an error in judgment, it appears it is at least in part because they have violated one or more of the basic principles psychologists working in this field for many years have identified as most effective for using intuition to guide major decisions (Exhibit 3.2 summarizes some of these key principles).[13]

Common errors that executives make involve *failing to be honest* (facing self-deception and pretense) and *attachment* (unwilling to let things be as they are rather than trying to make them be the way we would like them to be) about themselves and/or the decision they are about to make. Put another way, they engage in what psychologists commonly refer to as projection. Projection is the process whereby we cloud the intuitive cues we are able to receive as to what is in fact true by our own ego.[14] Hence, we transform reality into what we would like to be true instead of simply accurately perceiving what is in fact true. For example, in some cases particular executives may somehow become personally involved with a person about whom they have to make a management decision, and fail then to see the person objectively as he/she is vs. how they would like him/her to be. Or, they may not be completely receptive and open to the intuitive cues they are fully capable of receiving out of a fear that the intuitive picture accurately projected will not fit well with their own preconceived notion or preferred "reality."

Individual examples of executive responses are revealing in this regard. One top manager states:

Exhibit 3.2
Guidelines to Follow to Develop Your Intuition for Decision Making

• Intent	--	Value intuition and make the decision to develop your ability.
• Time	--	Devote time to developing it.
• Relax	--	Learn to release physical and emotional tension.
• Silence	--	Practice taking silent time alone for personal growth.
• Receptive	--	Be open to the internal cues you now receive.
• Honest	--	Recognize your own self-deception practices. Accept things as they truly are.
• Trust	--	Trust yourself and your internal cues.
• Courage	--	Be willing to accept and face the unknown openly.

Source: Constructed through a reading of the book by
          Frances E. Vaughan, Awakening Intuition (Garden
          City, NY: Anchor Books, 1979).

I can't recall any wrong decisions where intuition was the final step in the process. I have had situations where I failed to follow up on a feeling that "things weren't right" and made a decision which really screwed things up. At other times, I ignored the "hard nosed" rational assessment phase and allowed "wishful thinking" to control the decision.[15]

Another highly placed executive vice president of one of the largest corporations in America speaks of how the president of that same organization sometimes lets his own ego involvement cloud his normal ability to make sound decisions: "Sometimes he just gets too ego involved. He wants 100% on an issue when he could get 95% with a lot less grief. I've often had conflicts with him about his tendency to be this way."[16]

Executives admit that they also make mistakes when they violate these basic intuitive decision making principles: Relax before making a decision; allow adequate time for the decision to be made; and be centered and confident before making the decision. Exhibit 3.3 summarizes examples that executives actually gave. Typical statements are, "I've made mistakes when fatigue, boredom, or anger were present"; "My wrong decisions come when physical or emotional

Exhibit 3.3
Conditions That Impede the Use of Intuition

Not Honest with Self or Receptive	Not Relaxed
• Ego involved with question at hand. • Angry.	• Physical/emotional tension. • Fatigued, sluggish, or not feeling well.
Not Take Adequate Time	Not Trust Self
• Rushed to make decision. • Fail to get necessary background facts. • Fail to do homework required. • Act impulsively.	• Anxiety. • Fear. • Confused. • Not feel balanced. • Accommodate too much desires/feelings/arguments of others despite own feelings.

stress are present"; "Most things go wrong when I don't listen to myself"; and "When time pressure is there to make a decision. Supervisors or subordinates often just sit there expecting a decision right now."

Where Intuition Is Used in the Decision Making Process

We have seen thus far that top executives tested definitely feel that they consciously use their intuition to guide their most important decisions. They can identify a specific body of cues or indicators that they employ as guideposts for action, and this process has resulted by their own admission in very successful major decisions. At the same time, these executives state that when they make mistakes, it is primarily due to the fact that they fail to use their intuition effectively to guide their decisions. They allow themselves to get "off course" by letting other factors such as their own ego involvement get in the way of the normal flow of their intuitive radar.

What we have identified here then according to interview data is a decision making skill that top executives believe in and use to guide their most important decisions. If this is the case, do executives use their intuitive ability in the same way and at the same stage in their decision making process—or does it vary from executive to executive? The following question was asked in an effort to gather further insight as to how these highly intuitive executives might actually be using their skill: "How do you go about using your intuition to make your most important decisions?"

Their replies reveal that each executive is conscious of a methodology or system that works best for him/her. When examined as a whole, many executives share and use the same or a similar system—they activate their intuition in a similar manner and employ it at the same stage in their decision making process. But it is also true that several executives in the sample employ distinctly different techniques which vary from executive to executive. For this group, each decision maker has fashioned his/her own particular system custom designed to work for him/her. Each executive activates his/her intuitive ability in a unique way and employs his/her skill at different stages in the decision making process.

Many executives in the sample indicate that they use their intuitive ability like an *explorer*. When they are trying to make decisions that will affect their organizations' future, they seek to use their intuition to foresee the correct path to follow.[17] Under these circumstances, this group of executives is particularly careful to give their intuition "free rein." They are trying to generate unusual possibilities and new options that may not normally emerge from an analysis of past data or traditional ways of doing things. They find the most effective method for achieving this goal is not to adopt a rigid system or step-by-step method of decision making. What works for them is to allow their mind "to flow" where it wants to—making sense out of the various stimuli that come to it—whether sifting past experience or simply playing with concepts and ideas more heuristically. One executive describes the process this way: "The idea of a technique suggests to me a rigidity that chokes off intuition. My own intuition requires freedom, that can chew on all sorts of ideas and methods for nourishment."[18] Another top decision maker outlines his style this way: "I strive to be independent, non-conformist and non-traditional in the best sense of these terms. . . . This leads me to consider the possibilities of the unusual—in people and ideas."[19]

On the other hand, as noted earlier, a large number of respondents use their intuitive ability quite differently. They have a more structured decision making system that they routinely employ. It involves specific steps that are regularly followed—often including as the first step gathering and analyzing all the relevant data available concerning the problem at hand. Intuition in this system is used at *the back end vs. the front end* of the process—not so much as an explorer but rather as a *synthesizer* and *integrator*. This group of executives often insists on an adequate amount of time for incubation—the process of digesting and sifting through the information they have consumed before reaching their final decision.[20]

A key executive describes a typical example of this particular approach in this way:

I establish a clear, concise objective. I gather whatever information that is available, digest it, and if time is available, I allow a day or two for my intuition to work on it. An acceptable if not "the" answer has always evolved. The tougher the problem the shorter the time required for this process to work.[21]

These are the two major ways most respondents use their intuitive ability to make decisions. But there is also a third group of executives who have developed their own individual technique or system which might be termed *eclectic*. The method of using their intuitive ability to guide their decisions varies from individual to individual. For example, one respondent indicates that he uses his intuition to make an early judgment on issues before him long before an actual decision is required. But he does not cut off the flow of data input he receives pending the time when the actual decision must be made. Instead, he consciously cross-checks his initial "intuitive feel" for the course to take against the data constantly flowing to him until the actual decision is finally required. He states, "My initial intuitive decision turns out to be right greater than 75% of the time."[22]

Another executive in this group uses his intuition as a basis for delaying a final decision. He describes his process this way: "When the available options set off an internal signal which cries 'wrong,' I accept the need to give the decision more time. I start asking logical questions, and test my feelings of comfort/discomfort with the answers given."[23]

Techniques Executives Use to Activate/Facilitate Intuition for Decision Making

Whether the respondents use their intuitive ability for exploration, integration, or in an eclectic fashion, executives as a total group have found in common several specific techniques that serve to activate/facilitate the use of their intuition whenever they wish to use the skill for decision making. When asked, "When making a major decision, do you use any particular technique or method(s) to help draw on your intuitive ability more effectively?", these top executives volunteer a long list of techniques they find helpful (see Exhibit 3.4).

These techniques are summarized under the headings of *mental, relaxation*, and *analytical problem solving exercises*. What is worthy of note here is that this list coincides well with many of the techniques recommended by experts in the field of intuitional development. For example, Philip Goldberg's recent book, *The Intuitive Edge*, devotes three chapters to describing how to develop and use your intuition.[24] He recommends as an illustration "adopting a certain playfulness and an appreciation of whimsy." This is very similar to the top executives' actual practice of "playing freely with ideas without a specific goal in mind." Or, Goldberg recommends that your intuition will work more effectively in helping you solve your problem if you are precise about defining

Exhibit 3.4
Techniques and Exercises Used by Executives to Activate Their Intuition for Decision Making

Relaxation Techniques	Mental Exercises
• Clear mind mentally.	• Play freely with ideas without a specific goal in mind.
• Seek quiet times.	
• Seek solitude.	• Practice guided imagery.
• Listen to classical music.	Practice tolerating ambiguity and accepting lack of control.
• Sleep on problem.	
• Fast.	• Practice flexibility, openness to unknowns as they appear.
• Meditate.	
• Pray.	• Practice concentration.
• Drop problem and return to it later.	Try to think of unique solutions. Be willing to follow up on points that have no factual justification.
• Exercise.	
• Joke.	

Analytical Exercises
• Discuss problem with many colleagues who have different perspectives as well as respected friends.
• Concentrate on listening to not only what but how people express themselves.
• Immerse self totally in the issue at hand.
• Identify pros and cons; then assess feelings about each option.
• Consider problem only when most alert.
• Tune into internal reactions to outside stimuli.
• Analyze dreams.
• Insist on creative pause before reaching decision.
• Ask what do I want to do and what is "right" to do.

the problem you want solved. He advises as one technique writing out your thoughts and another of ''brainstorming with yourself''—allowing intuition to generate alternatives for you. His recommendations are very similar to the techniques these top executives actually use in their own decision making processes when they practice the mental and analytical exercises listed in Exhibit 3.4.

Use of Intuition Kept a Secret

Expert psychologists working in this field generally agree that an important vehicle for using and strengthening one's intuitive ability is to develop a *support group*—friends and colleagues with whom you can share the experience of using your intuitive skills.[25] However, executives are in large measure reluctant to engage in such practices. This is so at least in part because management training across the country in recent years has heavily emphasized the use of analytical management techniques almost to the total exclusion of other potentially useful skills and methods. Our own organizational and community culture has tended to reinforce this tendency.[26]

It is not surprising then to find that nearly half of the respondents, when asked the question, "Do you tend to 'keep it a secret' that you use intuition to make decisions, or do you feel comfortable sharing this fact with others?", indicate that they "keep it a secret"! One top female executive explains that revealing this fact would tend to undermine her effectiveness: "At work, I work with men; men who tend to regard the use of intuition as suspect, female, and unscientific. . . . If I revealed my 'secret', I'd have an even harder time persuading them to accept my suggestions."[27] She continues, "They wouldn't regard my ideas/decisions as being properly rational. Yet, they can justify the worst kind of screw-ups with a chart and a computer print-out."[28]

Many intuitive executives—whether male or female—would probably agree that she accurately describes the kind of organizational culture they all often have to face and endure. One male manager puts it this way:

I have tried explanations without success. Also, superiors seem to believe some sort of witchcraft or other dark art is being employed. Better to use it to advantage than go through the hassle of explanation. I've even gotten to the point of telling others I'm just a good guesser.[29]

Because intuitive executives often feel that their colleagues do not or will not understand that intuition can be a reliable basis on which to make important decisions, they often engage in elaborate games to legitimate the direction they propose taking. The decision is actually made on the basis of intuition, but the justification used is not. One top executive at one of the largest and most successful corporations in America put it this way: "Sometimes one must dress up a gut decision in 'data clothes' to make it acceptable/palatable, but this fine tuning is usually after the fact of the decision."[30]

Another typical response is not only illuminating but also instructive in that it points out the need for more theory and research on the process of using intuition in decision making:

I share this fact easily with other friendly intuitives, but try to disguise it as careful planning, research or an intellectual effort around others. This is not a matter of adopting a cunning strategy; those without the willingness/ability to use their own intuition are often frightened by intuitive demonstrations or reject any evidence not fitting their current paradigm. It's hard, however, for anyone to talk about intuition—we lack theory that also fits our rational body of knowledge.[31]

Practicing Techniques to Strengthen Present Intuitive Ability

Numerous experts on the use of brain skills for decision making recommend daily practice of a variety of specific techniques if one wishes to develop one's present intuitive ability further.[32] But, for all of the reasons we have already mentioned, such practice as a rule is not normally encouraged in organizations today. Even if an executive is aware that he/she has special skills in this area, the person is seldom encouraged to develop this talent further—or to learn how to do so on his/her own.

It is not surprising then to find even among the highly intuitive executives in this sample—who are conscious of their skill and who in fact use it to make their most important decisions—a certain reluctance to actively embark on a program designed to help them develop their present ability still further. When asked, "Do you use or practice regularly any particular technique or method(s) to help develop your intuitive ability further?", only one-third of the respondents indicated they do. For the group that does, Exhibit 3.5 summarizes the techniques they employ. It should be noted again that this list coincides well with methods often recommended for use by experts in the field of intuitive development.[33]

Of course, further research is required to demonstrate that the practice of such techniques is empirically effective for strengthening present intuitive ability. Tentatively, however, one might suggest on the basis of the actual verbatim responses received from the two-thirds who practice no expansive techniques at present that they might well benefit from further training. For example, several intuitive executives appear to believe that practice itself might somehow undercut or hinder their present ability. One manager openly asks, "If I practiced such techniques, would I still be intuitive?"[34] Several executives also acknowledge that they had never even thought about practicing any expansive techniques before being questioned about their decision making process. One respondent admitted, "I do not know how to develop my intuitive ability further,"[35] and another exclaimed, "I would probably benefit from a process that would let me build my effectiveness based on my intuitive sense."[36]

At the very least, executives in this group would probably benefit from workshops on this subject if for no other reason than to correct many of the misconceptions they presently hold/fear about their own intuitive ability and to bring them up to date on the most recent research in this field. It is also quite probable that if these executives were made more aware of some of the techniques that might be used to strengthen their present ability that they are not now aware

Exhibit 3.5
Techniques Top Executives Regularly Practice to Expand Their Intuitive Ability

Relaxation	Mental/Analytical
• Meditation.	• I Ching.
• Guided imagery.	• Mind mapping.
• Listen to inner self when relaxed.	• Read and attend psychic related events.
• Journal writing.	• Expose self to new ideas and situations outside
• Keep in good physical shape.	specialty.
	• Stay open and flexible.
• Pray, read Scripture.	
	• Read philosophy and
• Fast once a month.	philosophy of science.
	• Read science fiction.
	• Look for patterns where none appear to exist.
	• Keep notepad nearby for recording ideas/insights before they are forgotten and for further development.

of—and in a supportive setting—they could well make quantum strides in expanding their present capabilities still further.

CONCLUSIONS

The sample of top executives studied strongly believe that they use intuition as one of their skills to guide their most important decisions. They are able to clearly recall examples of such major decisions, their character and type, and the circumstances under which they were made. It also appears that these intuitive executives share a common body of cues that they use to help make, delay, or not make critical decisions. Many but not a majority of the executives in the sample regularly practice a variety of techniques to expand their intuitive skills— exercises that are similar to those recommended as effective by expert psychologists working in the field for several years now.

Much more research is required on the process of intuitive decision making among top executives before definitive conclusions can be reached. Tentatively, our research suggests that the effective use of intuition in management could well be a significant resource for increasing management productivity in the decade ahead. This is likely for several reasons. First, research on how the human brain functions is growing rapidly. Increasingly, processes such as intuition are being more clearly understood, as are methods for enhancing its effective use. As the mystery and magic of how intuition in fact works are dispelled through hard science research, the more likely executives are to understand, accept, and use this skill that we all possess to some degree.

Second, the research findings presented here suggest that even among highly intuitive executives, considerable opportunity exists for honing and developing their skills for more effective use. Executives admit to frequently making a variety of errors in their decision making processes which interfere with the natural flow and effectiveness of their intuitive ability. Further training to help eliminate these errors is likely to increase present productivity. Similarly, we have found that less than half of the top executives in the sample are willing to share with colleagues the fact that they use intuition to guide their most important decisions. They also spend time and resources "covering up" how they in fact often make these decisions.

It is suggested here that organizational productivity and job satisfaction could also be potentially increased if these top executives would instead focus their energy in a new and more innovative direction. Specifically, they could adopt a more positive attitude about their own intuitive ability, and take an active role in establishing support groups within their own organizations such as "intuition clubs" where skills and techniques could be shared and experimented with. They could also implement other similar programs whereby intuitive decision making processes could be quantified objectively and success records established. Sharing these findings could facilitate our better understanding of how intuition might best be developed and used in applied organizational settings likely to emerge in the decades ahead.

Assuming that you are an executive who would like to focus your energy in this new and more innovative direction, Chapter 4 will outline in some detail how you can now begin. You will learn how tests for intuitive ability can be used practically for more effective organizational management, and how you can begin a support network from within and outside your organization for expanding intuitive skills for practical decision making for today and tomorrow.

NOTES

1. The Appendix contains the actual questions asked in the survey. Based on the one hundred responses received, this questionnaire has been further modified and refined into a more structured survey instrument measuring intuitive management styles. See Weston H. Agor, *Test Your Intuitive Powers: AIM Survey* (Bryn Mawr, PA: Organization Design and Development, 1985).

2. Interview Respondent Number 3, 1984–85 Study.

3. Interview Respondent Number 46, 1984–85 Study.

4. Frances E. Vaughan, *Awakening Intuition* (Garden City, NY: Anchor Books, 1979), p. 4.

5. "Decision-Making Process," *Public Management* 65, 2 (February 1983), p. 17.

6. Interview Respondent Number 2, 1984–85 Study.

7. Interview Respondent Number 16, 1984–85 Study.

8. Interview Respondent Number 56, 1984–85 Study.

9. Interview Respondent Number 15, 1984–85 Study.

10. Interview Respondent Number 63, 1984–85 Study.

11. Interview Respondent Number 57, 1984–85 Study.

12. Marilee Zdenek, *The Right-Brain Experience: An Intimate Program to Free the Powers of Your Imagination* (New York: McGraw-Hill, 1983).

13. Vaughan, *Awakening Intuition*, pp. 202–5. Also see Tony Bastick, *Intuition: How We Think and Act* (New York: John Wiley & Sons, 1982).

14. Vaughan, *Awakening Intuition*, pp. 29–30. Also see her cassette tape, "The Intuitive You" (Washington, DC: American Psychological Association, 1982).

15. Interview Respondent Number 49, 1984–85 Study.

16. Interview Respondent Number 14, 1984–85 Study.

17. The technical term for this process is precognition. See, e.g., Charles T. Tart, *Altered States of Consciousness* (Garden City, NY: Doubleday & Co., 1972).

18. Interview Respondent Number 12, 1984–85 Study.

19. Interview Respondent Number 16, 1984–85 Study.

20. See Philip Goldberg, *The Intuitive Edge: Understanding and Developing Intuition* (Los Angeles: J. P. Tarcher, 1983), pp. 63–68.

21. Interview Respondent Number 3, 1984–85 Study.

22. Interview Respondent Number 2, 1984–85 Study.

23. Interview Respondent Number 24, 1984–85 Study.

24. Goldberg, *Intuitive Edge*, Chapters 8–10.

25. Vaughan, *Awakening Intuition*, p. 205.

26. Weston H. Agor, *Intuitive Management: Integrating Left and Right Brain Management Skills* (Englewood Cliffs, NJ: Prentice-Hall, 1984).

27. Interview Respondent Number 59, 1984–85 Study.

28. Ibid.

29. Interview Respondent Number 66, 1984–85 Study.

30. Interview Respondent Number 16, 1984–85 Study.

31. Interview Respondent Number 12, 1984–85 Study.

32. See, e.g., Jean Houston, *The Possible Human: A Course in Enhancing Your Physical, Mental, and Creative Abilities* (Los Angeles: J. P. Tarcher, 1982), and Roger N. Walsh and Frances E. Vaughan, eds., *Beyond Ego: Transpersonal Dimensions in Psychology* (Los Angeles: J. P. Tarcher, 1980).

33. See, e.g., Frances E. Vaughan's cassette tape, "Exercises for Awakening the Intuitive You," cassette number 20273 (Washington, DC: American Psycholocial Association, 1982).

34. Interview Respondent Number 29, 1984–85 Study.

35. Interview Respondent Number 66, 1984–85 Study.

36. Interview Respondent Number 24, 1984–85 Study.

PART II. Implementing a Program for Using and Developing Intuition to Increase Organizational Productivity:

CHAPTER 4. Using and Developing Your Intuitive Brain Skills

Investing time in learning how to use and develop intuitive brain skills could well be one of the most productive steps a top manager can take today. This is so for a number of reasons. First of all, top managers will be increasingly faced in this next decade with situations and settings that demand decisions unlike those experienced before. By their very nature, they will be difficult to analyze statistically. Traditional management techniques, though important and necessary, will not be sufficient to easily solve the problems at hand—or always clearly point which way to go.[1] As we have already seen in Chapter 3, intuition can be a useful brain skill to rely on under these circumstances.

Second, over this next decade, ongoing brain research is likely to uncover a growing range of techniques that top managers will be able to use to increase productivity dramatically. We can already say that we have learned more in this last decade about how the brain functions than in the whole previous history of man.[2] The future promises still greater quantum leaps in our ability to understand and use the greatest computer of all—the human brain. Beginning to put a program in place now to take advantage of this new knowledge—both on a personal and on an organizational level—is likely to generate high rates of return for the investment made.

There are clear signs that several top leaders around the world are already aware of this fact. For example, in Venezuela, brain skill development has become a major national goal under the direction of the minister of education, which has attracted the attention of several other country leaders.[3] In this country, a report of the Association of American Colleges in 1985 posits that every baccalaureate degree program should include training that enables a student to "recognize when reason and evidence are not enough, to discover the legitimacy of intuition, to subject inert data to the probing analysis of the mind."[4] A recent conference for senior public executives at the University of Texas at Austin featured the development of intuitive management skills because "we recognize that successful public executives must rely on a mix of intuition and disciplined analysis in their decision making.''[5]

Let us assume that you are one of those executives who is willing to focus your energy in this new and more innovative direction. While you see the value of many traditional management techniques to help guide decision making, you also see the potential for using intuition to dramatically increase productivity and job satisfaction—at both a personal and an organizational level. But perhaps you do not quite know how to go about realizing this potential for yourself or the organization you work with. Perhaps, like many of the top executives we just discussed, you have an abundant supply of intuitive skills, but you are reluctant to "try them out," to share your experiences with very many friends or colleagues, or to embark on a program for developing your ability further.

The most typical organizational setting I have encountered around the country is like this. Individual managers—and their organizations—already have the intuitive resources necessary to dramatically increase productivity! The key problem is that they do not know this is so. There are several reasons for this. First, top managers and their personnel/organizational development staff are normally not aware of the fact that techniques already exist for measuring intuitive ability. Second, usually no organizational routine or system is in place to consciously "go looking for" intuitive ability and then use the brain skill in an applied way to help solve management problems. Finally, it is rare indeed to find individual managers or organizations that are implementing programs designed to develop their intuitive talent further for various practical purposes.

The typical top manager today "knows" his/her colleagues primarily by job title, responsibility, or years of experience with the organization. Seldom do they "know" the same personnel in terms of brain skills and abilities except in the most casual ways (e.g., over the years, you have learned through experience that Joe or Jane is a "real good idea" person). The fact of the matter is that frequently top managers are not altogether clear on what their *own* brain skills are. They may have even practiced a particular management style for years that is totally inappropriate for the brain skills they have in greatest abundance.

It is not surprising then that blind spots develop at the individual manager level, on management teams, and in organizations as a whole. For example, a management team is normally put together primarily based on such criteria as job title and/or area of responsibility, years of experience, or because the boss likes the person (more often than not, because they think in the same way vs. in a complementary fashion). Seldom is the team or group formed guided first and foremost by brain skills that a person or group has that might be most appropriate for dealing with the task at hand. As a result, we often ignore or lose key talent—in this case intuitive talent—that is right before our very eyes to make use of and rely upon to help solve our most intractable management problems.

Most top managers and organizations today do not have the slightest idea who their most intuitive executives are either. Nor do the most intuitive executives in the organization usually know who each other are, and therefore how they might work to recombine their intuitive talent for problem solving more effectively. As we noted in Chapter 3, they may even be literally "hiding out" because they do not feel that openly using their brain skills will be well received and supported within the existing organizational culture. As a result, management may well be "flying blind" more often than they need to or than is really productive to do. Remember, highly intuitive executives as a rule have the "most effective human radar system" for seeing ahead precisely when "the road is unclear, and fog is rolling in over the hills."

METHODS TO HELP ALLOW INTUITION TO WORK FOR YOU

This chapter and Chapter 5 are designed for you—and executives like you. They outline a program that any top executive (or one aspiring to top management) can follow to more fully experience his/her own—and his/her organization's—intuitive potential. The program is designed to be practically useful *right now!* If implemented, personal and organizational productivity should increase within a very short period of time.

The program outlined in these two chapters is based on three major sources of data and information. The first and most important is what the top executives we have just discussed in Chapter 3 have taught me—whether through testing, interviews I have conducted with them, or a variety of other means.[6] The second is the large body of existing brain research and psychology literature from which several proven techniques are borrowed.[7] Third is the rich experience of working with a large variety of organizations in "hands-on" workshops, which has resulted in a product that can be effectively used for intuitive brain skill development.[8]

Become Cognitively Aware of Your Ability

One of the very first steps to take in any program designed to help use and develop the intuitive talent you potentially have is to learn cognitively which brain skills you already have yourself and within your organization! Frances E. Vaughan, Ph.D., psychologist, and one of the leading national experts on developing intuitive brain skills, puts it this way:

Awakening intuition is inseparable from the development of self-awareness. . . . Self-awareness is the foundation of psychological health and well-being. . . . You know better than anyone else in the world what you need. The problem in finding the answers you want is often not a lack of information but an unwillingness, or fear, of acknowledging what you already know.[9]

At a practical level, one move to make is to cognitively learn who you are (and your colleagues are) in terms of intuitive brain skills. Of what practical use is this? We know through research that intuitive managers are particularly good at performing certain kinds of tasks and functions, and these skills are particularly useful in certain occupational specializations and management levels (see Exhibit 4.1).[10] When we are faced with these kinds of situations in our own organization, would it not be useful to know where the best talent is to deal with these matters—irrespective of formal job title? Furthermore, it appears likely that problems highly intuitive executives tend to work best at (e.g., new idea generation, coping with change) are going to become increasingly prevalent in the management climate shaping the decade just ahead.[11]

If this is the case, is it not practically important to determine if your organization has the mix of brain talent appropriate for tomorrow's challenges vs. yesterday's? Would this information not also be potentially useful in designing training programs for existing personnel? At a personal level, would it not be helpful for you to learn your own mix of brain skills and assess how to develop the particular skills you wish to more effectively? Similarly, would this information not help you to determine how to select your own personal staff to ensure that their brain skills and talent complement yours?

Test Your Intuitive Powers: *AIM Survey*

One good way for you to cognitively get in touch with your brain skills is to take the *AIM Survey*. The results of the *AIM Survey* will indicate the present level of your intuitive ability and whether you are using this skill on the job to guide your management decisions. After you have scored and interpreted your results, you can also compare your scores to the national norms for highly intuitive managers, for your sex, ethnic background, and occupational specialty. The survey takes only about ten to fifteen minutes to complete, and consists of a total of twenty-six questions. This instrument also comes with a trainer's manual. Therefore, it is easy to administer throughout your organization with a minimum amount of effort.[12]

Your scores on the first part of the *AIM Survey* are plotted on a scale for intuition ranging from 0 to 12 (see Exhibit 4.2). A maximum score on either end of the scale is 12. Two scores on either end of the scale are possible—*intuitive* or *thinking*.[13]

If your highest score is *intuitive*, you have the ability to base your decisions on unknowns or possibilities. You have the potential ability to apply ingenuity to problems, to see how best to prepare for the future, and to tackle difficulties with zest. You are more likely to prefer management situations that are unstructured, fluid, and spontaneous. With a high score for intuition, you have the potential ability to function best in occupations that are characterized by crisis or rapid change and where you are asked to chart new, emerging trends from data including many unknowns. You also prefer to solve new and different problems vs. the same or similar problems time after time.

On the other hand, if your highest score is *thinking*, you have the ability to apply

Exhibit 4.1
Practical Use of Intuition in Organizations

Skills Possessed by Intuitive Manager	Management Situation Where Most Useful	Example Occupations Where Most Useful
Sees possibilities.	Top management.	Marketing.
Supplies ingenuity to problems.	Where there is rapid change or crisis.	Intelligence.
		Buying.
Can deal with and solve complex issues where data are incomplete.	Totally new trends are emerging in old field.	Counseling.
		Writers.
Furnishes new ideas.	Labor intensive organizations.	Sales.
Sees the future.		Nursing.
Motivates people to do the impossible.		Personnel/ Organizational development.
		Investments.
		Real estate development.

experience to problems, to bring up pertinent facts, to keep track of essential details, and to face difficulties with realism. With a high score for thinking, you have the potential to function best in occupations that demand ability to work logically; where attention to detail, procedures, and precision is valued highly; and where you are asked to implement existing policy usually made elsewhere.

If your intuitive and thinking scores are tied, you have the potential to rely on both feeling cues and factual cues to guide your decisions. However, there is the danger that you will have a difficult time making up your mind about the set of cues to which you should listen. Therefore, it is quite possible that you either will be slow in making critical decisions or will have difficulty making a decision at all without experiencing considerable stress (see Exhibit 4.3 for an overview of these two opposing brain styles in an organizational setting).

For our purposes here, we are most concerned with how you scored on this portion of the test first, and second whether your score appears to match well with the style you actually practice on the job. We are also interested to see how your intuition score compares with national norms for your management level, sex, occupational specialty, and ethnic background (see Exhibit 4.4).

The use of intuition appears to be a skill that is more prevalent as one moves

Exhibit 4.2
Plot Your Survey Results

```
                        Intuitive

                           12
                           --
                           --
                           --
                           --
                           --
                            6
                           --
                           --
                           --
                           --
                           --
                            0
                           --
                           --
                           --
                           --
                           --
                            6
                           --
                           --
                           --
                           --
                           --
                           12


                        Thinking
```

up the management ladder. As we noted in Chapter 2, top managers in every sample group tested scored higher than their subordinates on intuitive ability (6.5 mean score nationally). Bearing this fact in mind, recall again that John Naisbitt, the author of the best selling book *Megatrends*, predicts in his latest book, *Reinventing the Corporation*, that intuition "will gain new respectability" in the organizations of the immediate future.[14] Within this top management group, only 10 percent nationally can be classified as highly intuitive executives—their scores fall in the 10 to 12 range on the intuition scale. If your intuition score falls in this range, your ability ranks among the top 10 percent in the country.

As you will note in Exhibit 4.4, women score higher than men in intuitive ability. Similarly, available data also indicate that managers from an Asian ethnic background appear to have a higher level of intuitive ability than the average manager, followed by white and finally by black managers. Compare your scores to these results.

Finally, compare your score to national norms by occupational specialization

Exhibit 4.3
Brain Skills and Styles

Brain Skill Emphasized	Type of Organization Where Predominant	Task Preference	Problem Solving/ Decision Making Style	Example Applications	Sample Occupational Specialty
Thinking	Traditional	Routine	Deductive	Model building	Planning
	Pyramid	Precision	Objective	Projection	Management science
		Detail	Prefers solving problems by breakdown into parts, then approaching the problem sequentially using logic		Financial management
		Implementation			Engineering
		Repetitive			Law enforcement
					Military
Intuitive	Open	Non-routine	Inductive	Brainstorming	Personnel
	Temporary	Broad issues	Subjective	Challenging traditional assumptions	Marketing
	Rapidly changing	General policy options	Prefers solving problems by looking at the whole, then approaching the problem through hunches		Organization development
		Constant new assignments			Intelligence

Exhibit 4.4
Comparing Your Intuition Test Scores to National Norms

National Norms (Mean Scores)				Your Score
Management Level				
Top	Highly Intuitive Top		Middle/Lower	_____
6.5	10-12		5.8	
	Sex			
	Male	Female		_____
	6.3	6.9		
	Ethnic Background			
White	Black		Asian	_____
6.2	5.2		6.5	
Occupational Specialty				
Personnel	General Adminis- tration, Policy	Marketing, Sales	Finance, Military, Law, Law Enforce- ment	_____
7.9	6.7	6.3	4.9-5.1	

and by management level within occupations. As a rule, managers specializing in financial management, engineering, law, and law enforcement, e.g., have higher test scores on thinking vs. intuitive ability because these professions tend to place greater emphasis on facts and figures for decision making, value hierarchical models of management, and stress quantitative techniques of analysis. On the other hand, managers specializing in such fields as general administration or policy (likely to be the case for top managers), marketing and sales, and organizational development score higher on intuitive ability. This occurs because these fields tend to be characterized by elements of uncertainty and rapid change. Decisions often involve choices between shades of gray vs. black or white options. Intuitive skills in this context would appear to be particularly useful.

You now know whether you appear to be highly intuitive or not, how you compare with others in your sex, ethnic group, and occupational specialty. If you have administered this test within your office, division, or total organization, you also now know how you stand there. By completing the second part of the *AIM Survey*, you also know whether you are actually using your intuitive ability on-the-job to help guide your management decisions.

These test scores for you and/or your total organization can be used in a wide variety of ways. At the self-awareness level, one of the most effective ways to develop your intuitive ability further is to first of all have the cognitive awareness of who you are and how you compare with other colleagues. Let us assume for illustrative purposes that you score in the 10 to 12 range on the intuition scale— a score similar to that of the highly intuitive top executives we tested. You now have some idea of the level of your capability in this skill area compared to top managers nationally as well as national norms by sex, occupation, and occupational specialty. Since you know you have scored in the very top of the intuition range, a period of self-reflection should indicate to you that you have had a number of experiences over your lifetime at work and in your personal life like those of other highly intuitive executives I have interviewed nationally.

It is not uncommon among these executives to find that this brain skill often offers them a variety of cues that can serve as useful information in their decision making process. For example, some speak often of being able to finish word for word sentences of persons they care about deeply. Others tell of knowing that a close friend and associate is going to call before he/she actually does. Still others somehow get clear impressions and information about a person from a business handshake. A large and growing body of hard science research indicates that these and other similar experiences are common and much more widespread among the intuitive management community than was once thought to be the case.[15]

Think about these illustrative cases in this regard. Korn/Ferry International is a large executive recruitment firm with headquarters on the west coast. Lester Korn and Richard Ferry, the two kingpins of this successful organization, appear to have the capacity to communicate mentally with each other—even when words are not actually spoken.[16] Ponder the ability of Victor H. Palmieri, Stanley Hiller, Jr., and Sanford C. Sigoloff, three executives who specialize in corporate turnarounds guided by an uncanny talent for sizing up what is wrong at a company and then devising a strategy to fix it.[17] Or reflect on George Di Nardo, the senior vice president of information systems and research at Mellon Bank in Pittsburgh. This banking executive frequently pursues ventures that fly in the face of what others have done in the past with great success. When asked how he does this, he simply states that it comes from a sense he gets that he can accomplish it without any traditionally "hard factual evidence" that it can be done.[18]

The results from the *AIM Survey* give you one tool to cognitively think of yourself, your colleagues, and associates in a totally new way apart from traditional job titles and responsibilities and years of experience—namely, in terms of brain skills and styles. This new cognitive awareness of the intuitive brain skills that you have inside of yourself and your organization is one key to unlocking the door to increased personal and organizational productivity. As we shall see here and in Chapter 5, this process of cognitive self-discovery (i.e., how we think of ourselves and others) will in turn impact how much you are likely to start using your intuitive talent and working to develop it further. This information combined with other assessment tools (e.g., review of resumes, personal interviews, past job performance) will enable you to more effectively use your brain talent on organizational problems where it is likely to be most productive, and to help guide your colleagues and subordinates in a similar fashion.

The process is analogous to studying the top of an iceberg. *The intuitive brain skills that are likely to lead us to greater productivity are hidden below the water line!* As a result, we do not consciously work on using and developing our intuitive skills for applied use on-the-job. We do not normally have many programs within our organizations that try to match this talent to the management problems where it can best be used (e.g., networking with other intuitive talent to form management teams for creative problem solving). Productivity is lost as a result.

Practice a little introspective reflection now. Since you scored in the high range on the intuition scale, the following statements should characterize your present management style. Cognitively assess if this is indeed so.

Cognitive Awareness Exercise

- I am curious and independent. I tend to ask why not rather than why.

- My personal goals in life are determined first by setting my own priorities rather than being overly influenced by the external expectations of others.

- I particularly enjoy finding new solutions to old problems. But, I want to find the solution on my own without being told how to do so.

- I prefer an informal and relaxed management environment as compared to a formal or highly structured one.

You should also be able to cognitively identify with the traits outlined in Exhibit 4.5. You will note on the one hand that you have skills that are going to be highly valuable in the megatrend management climate American organizations are now entering.[19] At the same time, you are likely to have certain tendencies to watch for which should be carefully guarded against or balanced by thinking type managers who tend to have the opposite tendencies.[20]

Levels of Intuitive Ability

So far, you have learned a good deal about your intuitive brain skill and ability. But, there are several additional steps you can still take to expand further your own cognitive self-awareness. The highly intuitive top executives that I have tested and interviewed nationally appear to receive their cues on several different levels. The next step you need to take now is to become cognitively

Exhibit 4.5
Characteristics of Intuitive Managers

Characteristics of High Value	Tendencies to Guard Against
• good at generating new ideas. • good creative problem solver. • can make practical sense out of situations where data are limited. • can spot new emerging trends effectively.	• careless with details. • weak on follow-through and implementation of programs. • find routine and repetition difficult to handle. • tend to work in cyclical bursts of energy.

aware of the level(s) on which you receive your own intuitive cues. Broadly speaking, intuition functions on four different levels: physical, emotional, mental, and spiritual.[21]

At the physical level, intuitive awareness comes in the form of bodily sensations. Sometimes we have a strong body response to a person or situation when there is no apparent surface reason for having it. We simply know something without knowing how or why. Recent research indicates that we can be influenced by extrasensory stimulus even when we are not aware of it at the conscious level.[22] Put another way, our intuition is telling us what our body already knows to be true.

If you are experiencing a very stressful environment daily, e.g., your body is probably giving you numerous clues such as headaches or stomachaches. These clues may be translated practically into action in several ways: Alter the environment, remove yourself from the environment, or learn through stress reduction techniques how to handle the situation more effectively for your own long-term well being.

At the emotional level, intuitive signals are transmitted in the form of feelings. Surely many of us have had the experience sometime in our lives that we instantaneously liked or disliked someone we just met. Just feeling right or wrong about a situation or picking up visual cues about a person are good examples.

Third, intuitive cues can come to you on a mental level. This is when mentally you see a pattern or order to seemingly unrelated facts that may not be obvious to your colleagues just yet either. Albert Einstein attributed his theory of relativity to intuition—a flash of insight—not to a product of painstaking laboratory experiments and work with objective data. Charles Revson, the founder of Revlon, appeared to be able to operate effectively on this level when predicting what the future consumers of his product would be likely to want.[23]

Finally, intuition can function on a spiritual level. At this level, an executive will fully understand how his/her organization's acts are interlinked with all of humanity. At this level, one becomes aware of the meaning of the old biblical saying, "As ye sow so shall ye reap." Emphasis is on the transpersonal and the underlying oneness of life. At this level of awareness, you have the potential to tap into an energy force that Jean Shimoda Bolen, psychiatrist and author, describes as a "waking dream": "We sense there is an underlying meaning where we share a collective unconscious with humanity, where time and space become relative, and where, in the course of our everyday lives, we experience a nonordinary reality."[24]

The highly intuitive executives I have tested clearly make their most important decisions *operating on one or more of these levels of intuition.* Exhibit 4.6 summarizes the set of cues they receive classified by level of intuition. For example, one top management respondent states, "I just have a strong sense of knowing it's a right or wrong decision. When pressed for a rationale to support the decision, I frequently have to start an analytical procedure and construct supportive data or logic."[25] Other sample comments are, "Right decisions feel like a bolt of lightning or a sudden flash that this is the solution";[26] or "it is almost an automatic reaction as if I were responding to an unheard voice or a set of signals that even I cannot see. It's totally spontaneous. . . . It means it's something I should do."[27] These findings are consistent with a recent study among executives conducted by a Harvard University researcher. He found that there were clearly distinct physical reactions that executives experienced when making a correct intuitive decision as compared to one made by analytical processes. In the first instance, the heart would beat more rapidly and the palms would perspire, whereas in the alternative decision making situation these physiological changes were not experienced.[28]

On a physical level, some executives can touch a person or object and get valuable information they consider relevant to making a decision. Some high level managers such as the late President Lyndon Baines Johnson were famous for insisting on a personal interview, e.g., before making a critical decision for just this purpose. One of the managers I tested describes his skill on this level by relating this experience:

A few years ago, I had a position open in my office for a systems analyst who would work closely with other county offices, i.e., the treasurer, the auditor, the assessor, etc. I sent the young man to be interviewed by the various officials who were extremely impressed with him, his background and ability. When I talked with him after these interviews, something seemed wrong. I didn't know what it was, but my intuition told me to check on him further. I did and found he was a complete phony. I had nothing to go on but my intuition, and it served me well.[29]

Exhibit 4.6
Sample Cues Intuitive Executives Receive at Time of Important Decision

Physical	Emotional	Mental	Spiritual
sweat	enthusiasm	clear vision	unheard of signal or voice
anxiety	warmth	sense of knowing	
nausea	excitement	sudden flash	sense of conse-quence
fright	decisive	bolt of lightning	set of signals
queezy	calm/peaceful	know what will be said before is	metaphysical guide

Other managers work best mentally. They get their insights in isolation totally divorced from the stimulation of other people or outside objects. Jonas Salk, the inventor of the polio vaccine, is a good example here. Salk writes about his style of using intuition in his own book on the same subject in this way:

I do not remember exactly at what point I began to apply this way of examining my experience, but very early in my life I would imagine myself in the position of the object in which I was interested. Later, when I became a scientist, I would picture myself as a virus, or as a cancer cell, for example, and try to sense what it would be like to be either. ... When I had played through a series of such scenarios on a particular problem and had acquired new insights, I would design laboratory experiments accordingly.[30]

One of the executives I interviewed practices a very similar technique to that described by Jonas Salk:

I use coping rehearsal techniques. In many cases, it is the projection of imagery into possible problems that might come up, solving them or planning for them in my mind and then filing them away in case the situation ever comes up for a decision. That is, I anticipate possible upcoming decisions as far in advance as possible. This gives me time to plan realistic strategies for solving anticipated problems.[31]

Other highly intuitive executives try to function at the spiritual level. This may take on formal religious connotations or not depending on the executive in question. For example, Gulf Oil's chairman, James E. Lee, personally conducts prayers before every board meeting.[32] Or, take Dallas based real estate developer Trammell Crow, who has established such a reputation for honesty that "his handshake is better than a contract."[33]

Whichever level and technique work best for each executive, they each seem to have a good understanding of what works best for them. If you take the *AIM*

Survey mentioned earlier, the second part of the test will give you a good picture of how you actually use your intuitive ability and on which level(s) you receive your cues for decision making. It will also give you a base upon which to compare your personal experiences with or use of intuitive cues to those of other similar executives nationally. This process alone will not only help you to learn to feel more comfortable about your ability, but will also encourage you to openly share with other executives these experiences, and stimulate you to take conscious steps toward developing this brain skill still further for practical use.

Another way for you to become cognitively familiar with the different levels of your intuitive ability is to begin keeping an "intuition journal." Several of the top executives interviewed for this book state that they practice this technique, and find that it is also a useful vehicle to help them develop their brain skills still further. For example, a top executive of one of the most successful major corporations in America reveals:

I was discussing this with the president of the company the other day. We both have a note pad journal that we keep for ideas that come to us. . . . Lots of my best solutions come when I wake up in the middle of the night which I immediately write down. They "stand the light of day" later very well. It's *very clear* to me when these ideas come that they are good ones![34]

Exhibit 4.7 gives you a detailed outline of what to start recording in your intuition journal. This journal will give you a means for building a systematic record of your insights that can be used later for self-reflection, for checking the progress of your development, and also as a tool in channeling discussions with your colleagues. This record will help you to assess other related aspects of your intuitive development such as, for example, whether you seek to actively implement the intuitive insights you receive or whether you have adopted a style of simply ignoring them. This process can also be used to give you other assistance such as how you might actually be blocking your underlying intuitive ability from coming through to serve you.

Record in your intuition journal such information as how and when your cues and insights come to you, by what means (i.e., by level of intuition and specific cues such as through dreams), and check their apparent accuracy. Note whether you appear over time to have a particular pattern. See if one particular level of intuition seems to be your forte, and other similar matters. Noting and assessing all these things will help you to get a better understanding of how you function best. Recent research has shown, for example, that we can facilitate the process of intuitive development if we learn to understand and work with the skill openly in this way.[35]

Other cognitive techniques can also be used to help you learn productively about other aspects of your intuitive ability as well as to cross-check and compare with the findings from using the instruments already described. For example, although we have identified so far a number of ways in which intuitive managers

Exhibit 4.7
What to Record in Your Intuition Journal

Level of intuitive experience

- Physical

- Emotional

- Mental

- Spiritual

Accurate intuitive experiences

- Examples

- Level used

- Conditions/circumstances (e.g., time, events, people involved, own emotional state, etc.)

"Inaccurate" intuitive experiences

- Examples

- Level used

- Conditions/circumstances (same as above)

- Record other possible factors operating which might have interrupted intuitive flow (e.g., projection, ego involvement)

Other experiences

- Sharing with support group members

- Success/failure with practice techniques

are similar, it is also true that they have dissimilar characteristics that are important to note and be aware of. One of the most important characteristics in this regard is extroversion vs. introversion (see Exhibit 4.8). Extroverted intuitives are able to activate and use their ability in quite different ways in organizational settings than is true for introverted intuitives. Knowing which type you are in this regard is also very helpful information to have. It will give you a better cognitive understanding of circumstances in which you are likely to be able to function best in a management setting and also where you will have difficulty. If you have a similar understanding of your colleagues or subordinates, it will give you guidance as to how to best search out and make use of the intuitive talent that you have available to you.[36]

One of the best instruments available to you for getting an in-depth assessment

Exhibit 4.8
Management Style of Extroverted and Introverted Intuitive Managers

EXTROVERTED INTUITIVE	INTROVERTED INTUITIVE
Expresses self naturally and easily, works easily with others.	Finds self-expression difficult, prefers to work more alone.
Most effective in the promotion and initiation of new enterprises.	Most effective in promoting understanding and interpreting life experiences.
Uses inner awareness to understand how to approach a situation.	Uses a situation to get better inner understanding.
Enthusiastic at onset, but sometimes fails to follow through on activities or details.	Has difficulty persuading others to see clear answers or to implement them practically.
Insight comes through personal interaction and/or touch.	Insight comes through mental processes.

Source: Table is constructed from a reading of
           Isabel Briggs Myers and Peter B. Myers,
           Gifts Differing (Palo Alto, CA: Consulting
           Psychologists Press, 1980).

of both your intuitive ability and also your personal style in using this brain skill along the dimension of extroversion–introversion (as well as two others) is the MBTI.[37] The advantage of using this particular instrument is that it has a long track record of reliability and validity spanning more than forty years. Another advantage is that there is an extensive literature available on how to practically use the survey results in a wide variety of organizational settings.

Another newer instrument which appears to hold great promise is the Singer–Loomis Inventory.[38] Based in part on the MBTI, the advantage of this particular instrument is that it seeks to measure how you use your intuitive ability (among other skills) on a *situational* basis. Hence, in one setting, for example, you might be quite comfortable acting as an extroverted intuitive might while in another more as an introverted intuitive would. If you need to have this degree of sensitivity in your overall cognitive assessment program, this instrument will help you to acquire it.

Handwriting analysis is still another cognitive assessment tool that can be used for determining your level of intuitive ability as well as a broad range of other characteristics such as analytical skills and management styles.[39] Finally, reading about the experiences of other intuitive executives is another safe way to gain a better cognitive sense of your intuitive ability. You will be surprised to find that what is happening to you has already happened to other executives many times. You will also learn to profit from their experiences—to find other ways to recognize and tap into your ability—and to apply it day-to-day to help guide your decisions. This book and the books by such successful scientists and inventors as Jonas Salk and Buckminster Fuller who describe how their intuitive processes work might be good places to start.[40]

Practice Your Intuitive Ability

Now that you have become more fully aware of the various aspects of your intuitive ability, the next most important step you can take is to *practice regularly* using the brain skill you have learned so much about. This should be done both alone and in a group context. The advantage of individual practice sessions is that they allow you to follow freely where your own mind takes you, and under circumstances and settings that are most comfortable to you—privately without interruption or fear of sanction/reprisal. Another advantage of working alone at times is you can experiment with a variety of techniques and settings to explore what might work for you. Some of these might not be either comfortable or feasible to carry out in a group setting. Another reason is that you may simply be just beginning to learn about your intuitive talent. You may not really know what will or will not work for you—or when. While you are all alone, you have the freedom you need to openly explore the full range of alternatives that are available to you, and at your own pace. Finally, working alone will probably help you to more easily develop the level of confidence you need before you begin openly sharing and working with this brain skill in a group.

When all is said and done, however, one of the major reasons for you to practice this brain skill is in order to "bring it on line" on command for applied use in organizations. Therefore, ultimately it will also be beneficial to practice developing your skills in group settings too—both applied and not applied. Here you will also learn some new lessons about your ability, such as how to develop a "group intuitive energy," how individual intuitive input can be engineered in the group to accelerate a problem solving process, and how to use your ability along with other personality traits so that you can effectively articulate in the group what "you know to be true" and persuade the group that you are indeed correct.

What follows here are sample exercises you can practice, which are designed for use on either the individual or the group level as indicated.

Exercises to Practice Alone

Here are a group of exercises for you to consider practicing on your own. They are particularly useful for working on the list of guiding principles for strengthening your intuitive ability outlined in Exhibit 3.2 (e.g., time, silence, receptive, and courage). Try the exercise you feel most comfortable with first and gradually move on to others later. You may even want to try eventually developing your own series of exercises to practice.

Getting Lost on Purpose

Go alone to a totally new town or rural location that you are not familiar with. Do not take a map or compass or other device for assistance. Get lost on purpose. Now, "feel" your way back home. Avoid asking other people for directions or assistance. Try to avoid using traditional landmarks like the stars for guidance. Instead, focus all of your energy on your own inner resources—your own sense of direction. Now go home.

Take a Risk

Take a risk—something you would normally avoid doing.[41] It is up to you what you pick. It can vary from trying to consciously face a fear you know you have (e.g., taking a high altitude ride because you know you fear heights) to trying a new experience (e.g., if you are a single woman, asking a man out on a date when you never have before). Focus on yourself now. What do you feel at the thought of taking this step? At what intuitive level? How do your feelings change as you go through this process? Reflect on yourself once the experience is over. Would you now be willing to repeat this experience? Why or why not? What do these reactions tell you about yourself?

Church Hop

Whatever your particular religion or philosophical orientation, set about to "church hop" to every major church or religious group in your (or another) community over the next several weekends. Expose yourself to all the possible philosophies, approaches, services, and other functions that you can. As you do so, reflect on how you feel as you proceed. Ask yourself how you react to the things you see and hear. Ask yourself, "How does what I believe now get affected by the way I *control* the cues I am willing to receive or expose myself to?" Once you have completed this exercise, reflect on what you are feeling like now compared to when you started the exercise. How have you changed? Why? How will this new awareness affect what you do in the future, what you are willing to experience in the future—whether it be religious or otherwise? It might be useful now to ponder this question, "Knowing what I now know, seeing what I have now seen, taking the best of all those experiences I have just had, how would I build a new church just for me?"

Guided Imagery and Meditation Tapes

Find a comfortable room or location for yourself where you will not be interrupted. Select some of the cassette tapes recommended in the annotated bibliography at the back of this book. Experiment with the different types of tapes there and also with different times of the day for practice. Learn to identify with techniques that seem comfortable to you and to which you respond. Also learn the times of the day and other situational factors that affect your intuitive ability the most. I have experimented with all of the tapes recommended personally and also in executive workshop sessions. What is very clear from this process is that each individual responds to the same tape in different ways. Hence, in the final analysis, you must find the approach that works best for you.

For example, you will find that some of the cassette tapes recommended contain only quiet music (e.g., harp and piano) while still others have sounds from the ocean surf or the open countryside. Still others have verbal scripts that guide you step-by-step within yourself to work on your intuitive self. From the workshops I have conducted nationally, I note that introverted intuitives tend to prefer tapes that have only music or sounds whereas extroverted intuitives appear to respond to verbal guidance more often. Assuming you have completed the cognitive testing I recommended earlier, you might wish to select at the beginning the tape that is most likely to appeal to you.[42]

Computer Games

There have been several software games recently (or soon to be) released on the market that you can use to practice your intuitive ability. Depending on which package you choose, you can work on different aspects of your ability (e.g., precognition, which is the ability to anticipate the future; or remote viewing, which is the capacity to describe the situation and setting where a distant person is located). Again, consult the bibliography at the back of the book for further guidance.[43] Here I will describe just one of these computer games developed by Alan Vaughan, a highly intuitive person who uses his skills professionally for a number of clients.[44]

This computer game will help you to work on and develop your precognitive ability—a skill that will certainly be a premium in the rapid change settings you as a manager are now facing. The software package for the game is designed for use with an Apple IIe microcomputer. Here are the steps to take.

- Turn on the computer and load the software program.
- Read the game instructions. The task is to guess the number that is being randomly generated by the computer accurately *before* the computer actually does so. If you guess correctly, you will score a hit and get a certain number of points. If you guess wrong but close to the target, you will get a smaller number of points. If your guess is far from the target, you will not get any points.

  The target is round like a clock and divided at first into six sections. If you score enough points to go on, the game becomes more difficult, with the target then divided into first twelve and finally eighteen sections. You may move the clock dial either clockwise or counter-clockwise. When you think you know in what section of the clock dial the actual number will be that the computer will then generate, you hit the computer key that records your choice.
- Start the game.

- Move the dial clockwise or counter-clockwise.
- Note which direction seems to feel most comfortable to you. Also note whether you experience other sensations (e.g., do you feel like a gravity force is pulling you when you get near the correct piece of the dial?).
- Practice your different levels of intuitive awareness (i.e., physical, mental, emotional, spiritual). Become aware of which level works best for you (e.g., track the dial with your hand touch; close your eyes and try to track the dial mentally; try both at the same time).
- Notice whether your score improves with practice and whether this is linear or curvilinear.
- Do other techniques practiced before this exercise help you to score better (e.g., meditation)?

Create Your Own Exercise

Once you have practiced several of the techniques and exercises already recommended, you might now want to create your own exercise or game. It can be related to solving a management problem you have at hand in your organization that you want to solve—or it could be totally unrelated to work. How you design the exercise and what you experiment with in the way of techniques are entirely up to you. You are free to choose, to experiment, to fail, to learn to run—whatever, just as long as you have made the basic commitment to try practicing your intuitive ability.

Exercises to Practice in a Group Setting

These exercises are designed to help you learn more about on which intuitive level(s) you function best (physical, emotional, mental, or spiritual), and also to help you learn how to bring this level(s) "on line" when needed to solve management problems (e.g., who to recruit or hire, how to work most effectively together, or how to motivate a person to work more productively). Some will work best if practiced with colleagues at work that you have just met for the first time or have seen only infrequently.

Face to Face

Follow these steps:

- Sit in two chairs facing each other.
- Relax and quiet the mind (taking three or four deep slow breaths will probably help to do this).
- Take turns "reading" what you think the other person is like—his/her strengths and weaknesses.
- Practice using each of the different levels of intuitive awareness to do this (e.g., close your eyes first with no eye or hand contact; then open your eyes first but still with no hand contact; then add hand contact, etc.).

- Exchange with each other the images that have come to your mind.
- Seek verification.
- Become aware of what types of information you receive and on what level. Also become aware of other processes (e.g., do added time and concentration seem to produce more information for you or do you seem to lose contact after a period of concentration?).
- Try the same exercise mixing the sexes.
- Become aware of whether this alters your intuitive flow and reflect on what this tells you about yourself.
- Practice this exercise several times with several different colleagues now.
- Become aware of what else you now learn (Do you get more or less effective with practice? What other variables seem to facilitate or interrupt your intuitive flow?).

Supervisor–Subordinate

This exercise is designed to force you back to your own intuitive self and the intuitive self of your subordinate by altering the traditional way you have come to interact. By giving each other permission to exercise your own intuitive selves, you learn how to function more productively; the potential for still greater performance in the future is unlocked; and job satisfaction is also enhanced.

Follow these steps:

- Start with thirty minute exchanges made up of fifteen minutes each.
- Pick one of your direct subordinates.
- Face each other in a sitting position. Hold hands and close your eyes. Relax and concentrate now.
- Focus your mind on words like *cooperation, support, help,* and *assistance.*
- You as supervisor ask your subordinate this simple question, "How do you feel I can perform my job more effectively?"
- Reflect for a few moments on the answers given.
- Reverse the process with the subordinate asking the same question.
- Subordinate now reflects for a few moments on the answers given.
- Each of you now thanks the other person for his/her suggestions. Promise to reflect more on these suggestions and to meet again the next week.
- Meet the next week with each person freely outlining what he/she has accepted or rejected and why.
- Repeat the process once more the following week.
- Each person now exchanges with the other what he/she has learned about himself/ herself first, and then about the other person second.
- Agree to meet and carry out this exercise again once a month in the future and to keep a written record of the results for possible use and exchange throughout your organization.

Exchange Intuitive Experiences at Work

This exercise is designed to help you develop your skills further by becoming more confident about exchanging the intuitive experiences you have had at work, and to become more fully aware of the fact that productivity can be enhanced by this exchange.

Follow these steps:

• Pair with a colleague at work that scores as high on the intuitive ability scale from the *AIM Survey* as you do.

• Each of you should freely discuss intuitive experiences that you have had that relate to your work in recent years.

• Become aware of the type of experiences you have had (type, level, when they come to you, etc.).

• Note their similarities and differences with those of your colleague. Also reflect on what you have learned by this exchange (e.g., techniques the other person used that you might try also; lost productivity because you each kept your intuitive insights a secret up to now, etc.).

• Note how you feel after this process of sharing (e.g., more confident, excited, creative).

You might wish to consider formalizing this experience throughout your organization (we will discuss this further in Chapter 5). One of the benefits of my own work on intuition over the last five years is that I have grown through similar exchanges with my colleagues. New doors and techniques have opened more rapidly to me as a result than I could ever have achieved by simply working all alone. Simply said, this process serves only to enhance both our personal/ group productivity and job satisfaction.

Individual in the Middle

This exercise like "Face to Face" and "Supervisor–Subordinate" is designed to help you learn and practice on which intuitive level(s) you and the group as a whole function best, and to learn how to jointly create the group energy necessary to bring this ability "on line" when needed to solve common problems where this brain skill can be practically useful (such as therapy, counseling, motivation, and problem solving).

The key difference between this exercise and the other ones mentioned so far is that this one will help you and the work group to learn how individual intuitive energy can be combined together to form a group intuitive energy that is *synergistic* (i.e., the whole group energy level achieved is greater than the sum of the individual intuitive parts). Once individual participants and the group as a whole learn how to create this synergistic energy in dealing with/solving personnel problems, it can be strengthened through the practice of the other exercises below, and laterally transferred to help solve parallel organizational management problems.

Follow these steps:

• Have the person to be "read" sit in a chair in the middle of a circle surrounded by the other members of the group.

- Relax and quiet the mind using the breathing technique already mentioned.

- Each member of the group in the circle should now hold hands so that the circle is completely unbroken. Close your eyes.

- Practice a brief meditation exercise that you are all comfortable with using.

- Relax in total silence. Notice now how you feel. Sense how the group together has seemed to stimulate your intuitive powers. Note the levels on which insights are coming to you and in what form (i.e., pictures, phrases, etc.).

- At will, take turns "reading" the person in the middle. Note how the individual insights overlap but also complement each other.

- After one round, relax while one member of the group records all of the insights given and verification is sought from the person in the middle.

- Repeat now the focusing exercises above.

- Begin another round of "readings," but this time with one distinct difference. First, each person should touch the individual in the middle and then report the insights gained. Next, open your eyes and look at the person—reporting the additional insights gained. Note how you feel at each round in this process. Do you sense any particular type of energy flows or shifts? What seems to make them happen? How do they affect your intuitive powers to address the "reading" at hand? How do you now feel about other members in the group (e.g., closer, more distant)?

- Now relax, and again have one member of the group record the additional set of insights given and seek verification from the person in the middle.

- Have everyone now join the group circle.

- Openly discuss this total experience, what was felt and the various *individual* impressions gained. Reflect on what you have now learned—as an *individual* about your own skills and as a *group*.

Take a Common Management Problem to Solve

Once you have completed the exercise above, take any management problem you wish to solve at work such as "How can we increase output next year?", "What should our major products be in 1990?", or "How should our company health program be reorganized?" Now focus on that problem as a group just as you did on "reading" one of your group colleagues. Follow the same steps and recording intervals to begin with. Perhaps later you will wish to try experimenting with a slightly different format such as taking a week or several days between each group session before again returning to the same problem.

Whichever format ultimately used or experimented with, become aware of how your individual and group energy changes as each alternative technique is tried. Also note how the energy changes over time as you continue to work as a group together. At the end of the process, take time to reflect on and acknowledge the new energy you have created. Reflect on the question, "Why did we not solve problems this way before?"

Success via Synergy

This is a particularly useful exercise to run right after your group has just completed solving an applied problem like the one outlined above. It is designed for use here to reinforce the principles of synergy just learned and experienced first hand. It is also designed to again force members of the group within themselves to reflect on how they use intuitive brain skills for decision making (at both an individual and a group level), and to give thought to ways in which they can enhance their personal and group capacity to make important decisions more productively.

Follow these steps:

• Distribute to the group the test instrument *Success via Synergy*.[45]

• Ask each person to take the test and self-score the results.

• Now ask all members to relax and replay in their mind the game they just played, "Take a Common Management Problem to Solve."

• Play a meditation tape while they are doing so.

• Once this step has been completed, ask them to reflect on how their scores on the test *Success via Synergy*, which measures personal characteristics conducive to creating this group energy, might be linked to how they actually performed in the applied exercise above.

• Again play a brief meditation tape to assist them in their reflection process.

• After this step is completed, open the session to whatever comments and exchange the members wish to now make.

Create Your Own Group Games

As with the exercises you developed for practice while alone, you can also benefit from developing your own group exercise for practicing your "group intuitive ability." As before, how you design the game and what you experiment with in the way of techniques are entirely up to you.

For example, you might wish to use your *AIM Survey* scores to form two groups at work—one highly *intuitive* and one highly *thinking* based on their test results. Start with the "Common Management Problem to Solve" exercise and steps outlined above, and ask each group to separately work on it, developing two group lists of proposed solutions. Next, come back together as one joint group and share your respective lists. Finally, form one group list of proposed solutions after practicing the meditation exercises outlined above.

Once you have generated a final group "list of recommended solutions," discuss as a group what you have learned along the way at each stage in the process. Reflect on what you have learned from your "peer brain types" and also what you have learned from your "brain opposites." Examine the content and scope of the "recommended list of changes" that was proposed at each stage in the exercise. Note how it changed, how the respective groups' lists complemented each other's, and how each list overlapped in some ways. Reflect also on how you—and all the groups—have changed. What have you learned about yourself? Be sure to also take stock of your individual and group productivity level at this point. How has it changed in terms of both quality and quantity?

BRAIN SKILL MANAGEMENT PROGRAM

Thus far in this chapter, we have discussed ways in which you can use and develop your intuitive ability for applied use in day-to-day management. The implications are that you can use this information to design and guide the implementation of an overall *brain skill management* (BSM) *program* in your organization that will help to increase productivity as well as job satisfaction.

You have learned here a totally new way of seeing yourself and your colleagues apart from the traditional job titles and responsibilities or years of experience— namely, in terms of *brain skills* and *styles*. Here are some examples of how you can use brain skill testing and assessments in a practical way to increase productivity.

The scores obtained from the *AIM Survey* can be used as one means of identifying the *creative resource potential* that exists inside of you and your own organization which is available for use and further development. These data combined with other assessment tools (e.g., review of resumes, personal interviews, past job performance) will enable you to design specific programs for more effectively using this brain talent on organizational problems where the skill is most likely to be productive (see Exhibit 4.9). When referring to intuitive brain talent, it has been my experience that all too often we do not have a good sense of the degree to which we possess this talent—personally or in our own organizations. For example, efficiency experts spend a good deal of time studying how effectively we use traditional analytical skills, but normally ignore the measurement of less visible intuitive brain skills. This process is analogous to studying the top of an iceberg. The management resource that is most likely to lead us to greater productivity is hidden below the water line! As a result, we do not consciously work on using and developing intuitive skills for applied use on the job. We do not normally have many programs within our organization that try to match this talent to the management problems where it can best be used. Productivity is lost as a result. This is a real opportunity for you to now take advantage of!

Existing research that we have discussed demonstrates that highly intuitive executives are particularly skilled at generating totally new approaches to solving existing problems in brainstorming sessions. They also prefer informal and more relaxed styles in management (see Exhibit 4.10). When you or your organization is faced with situations like these (e.g., assess the impact of technology on the future direction of an organization), using your own and your organization's intuition test profiles would be one way to custom build the most effective team or problem solving group capable of addressing this issue as well as designing the particular organizational style to use when the group actually begins to work

Exhibit 4.9
Management Setting Where Intuition Is Most Useful

Situation	Method to Use
Problem solving	Use intuition along with reason to come up with integrated solution that is both visionary and practical.
Future projections Meeting crises	Explore alternative actions with limited or inadequate information at hand, pick the option that <u>feels</u> most possible and also practical.
Team building	Use test results to build the team types that can best solve different problems at hand.
Organizational design Management	Use test results, work experience, and own feeling to decide how to lead meetings, write memos, organize a room, communicate between departments, and pick personal staff.

Exhibit 4.10
Common Traits, Skills, and Management Styles of Intuitive Executives

Traits	Skills	Management Styles
Good self-image.	See possibilities.	Informal.
Curious.	Can furnish new ideas.	Focus on solutions.
Independent.	Supply ingenuity to problems.	Work at several tasks at once.
Inner vs. outer directed.	Comfortable with complexity and imponderables.	Prefer not to be told how to complete a task.
Prefer action vs. inaction.	Can provide the spark to make the impossible happen.	Uncomfortable with routine and rules.
Take risks.		

Exhibit 4.11

Using Intuition Brain Scores to Help Prepare Your Organization for the Future

- Recruit, place, and develop personnel by management level and occupational specialty including career changes, adaptation to organizational changes such as mergers, outplacement.

- Create teams that can solve problems on a situational basis (e.g., crisis, intelligence).

- Assess future trends and implications for management.

- Assess, locate, and develop creative potential in organizations.

- Generate and make a practical assessment of creative ideas and/or new policy proposals.

- Understand and overcome communication problems including sex role stereotypes and cultural differences.

- Assess and manage stress.

- Develop and implement training programs.

- Develop workable employee compensation and benefit programs.

on the issue. In this particular case, weight should probably be given in selection to high *AIM Survey* scores on intuition, e.g., and then allowing this group to practice a more "free wheeling" work style and wear more informal clothing at work. This approach would probably be most conducive to actual performance on-the-job.

Another potential use of intuition test scores is to help guide the design and development of overall organizational development and transformation programs (see Exhibit 4.11 for illustrations). For example, let us say that you are a top executive in one of the regional Bell telephone companies nationally. Recent changes in deregulation have significantly impacted your organization. You foresee that you are going to need to have a different mix of talent in the future than you presently have internally—and/or present personnel are going to require considerable retraining to adapt to these new emerging trends. You also recognize that increased competitive pressure will demand that new/existing personnel are going to have to operate even more productively in the future.

Intuitive test scores (along with other assessment resources) can be one useful tool under these circumstances to guide the change process. One specific target could be realizing the best possible match between your personnel's brain skills/ management capabilities and the new job specifications being developed within your organization. This could be achieved, in part, by collecting intuitive test scores by individual and comparing them to both the position the person is presently working in and the new positions being designed now. This process might help you to identify the best candidates among existing personnel for the new positions and responsibilities emerging. Another outcome might be that your organization and/or the individual being tested discover intuitive brain skills and abilities among existing staff that were not known or properly utilized. These persons may well be more productively used in the future. Maybe you will also find that potential intuitive ability is identified for applied use, but found to be presently blocked and subject to training. Still another conclusion might be that a search for different personnel outside the existing staff is required to meet the present/future needs of the organization. Whatever the specific conclusions/actions generated by this stage in the organization development/transformation program, training or retraining needs are likely to be identified for implementation. The goal of training would be for individual managers and the organization as a whole to achieve the most complete use of all *existing* and *potential* brain skills possible.

Finally, it was mentioned earlier that one of the most effective ways for using and developing your (and your organization's) intuitive ability further is to know cognitively something about the talent you may have within. An awareness of our own talent can have a major impact on how we think of ourselves, and how we think of ourselves will in turn impact how much we are likely to start using our intuitive talent and working to develop it further. Similarly, knowing who and where your "like types" are in an organization is likely to be an important first step necessary for creating support networks where your talent can comfortably be shared and developed for organizational use.

Responses I have received from the top group of executives tested are clear cases in point. For example, one highly intuitive top manager who scores in the 10 to 12 range on my intuition scale clearly does not think of himself as being highly intuitive. He states, "On the chance that you are not pulling my leg that I scored in the top 10%, I'm returning your questionnaire."[46] It is suggested based on the extensive work I have done with executives internationally that this top official has real talent that is often "hidden below the water line," and perhaps too infrequently used. I also suggest to you that as his self-concept about his intuitive talent changes, and as he learns to be more comfortable about sharing it with his colleagues, the more likely he will be able to bring this brain skill "to the surface" and on line for more productive use. Finally, I suggest to you our pattern of thought and the extent to which we use our underlying intuitive ability are often culturally conditioned and reinforced within our organizations— usually to the detriment of higher productivity and job satisfaction. Helping to create an environment within your organization where intuitive talent can be openly used and developed is a significant leadership opportunity for you.

Turn now to Chapter 5 where I will outline how you can use what you have learned so far to lead your organization step-by-step toward increased productivity through the applied use of intuitive brain skills.

NOTES

1. Under these new emerging circumstances, other more intuitive techniques have proven to be more useful. See, e.g., David Loye, *The Knowable Future: A Psychology of Forecasting and Prophecy* (New York: John Wiley & Sons, 1978) and David Loye, *The Sphinx and the Rainbow: Brain, Mind, and Future Vision* (Boulder, CO: Shambhala, 1983).

2. See, e.g., the public television series, "The Brain" (Wilmette, IL: Annenberg/CPB Collection, 1984), and the special issue on the brain in *Psychology Today* (November 1985).

3. For details on this country's effort and that of others, see "Tarrytown Meeting," *Leading Edge Bulletin* 4, 15 (June 4, 1984), p. 3.

4. *Integrity in the College Curriculum: A Report to the Academic Community* (Washington, DC: Association of American Colleges, 1985), p. 15.

5. "New Times, New Strategies," paper given at the Public Executive Institute (Austin, TX, July 12–20, 1985).

6. Over 3,000 executives have now been tested nationally, of which 100 highly intuitive executives have been tested or interviewed in great depth. Workshops that I have conducted in the United States and abroad have been another vehicle. This process has been particularly useful because it has enabled me not only to experiment with various techniques and assess their impact, but also to talk to these executives in some depth during informal settings where they are more willing to reveal privately some of their intuitive experiences that they are often unwilling to share with their colleagues.

I am reminded in this regard of a long dinner conversation in 1983 with the president of a west coast firm after I gave a preconference workshop at the 1983 Annual Organizational Development Conference in Pasadena, California. He told me that when there were problems in his organization, he could often determine what the solution was "just by walking around, touching the papers on the desks in the offices and shaking hands with some of the executives." He said later, "Sometimes they think I'm nuts around the home office." Gifted maybe, but hardly nuts, my research suggests.

7. See the annotated bibliography at the back of this book as well as the specific citations made in this chapter and Chapter 5.

8. For details, see the brochure *ENFP Enterprises* (El Paso, TX: ENFP Enterprises, 1985).

9. Frances E. Vaughan, *Awakening Intuition* (Garden City, NY: Anchor Books, 1979), p. 180.

10. See, e.g., Isabel Briggs Myers and Peter B. Myers, *Gifts Differing* (Palo Alto, CA: Consulting Psychologists Press, 1980).

11. John Naisbitt, *Megatrends: Ten New Directions Transforming Our Lives* (New York: Warner Books, 1984); also John Naisbitt and Patricia Aburdene, *Reinventing the Corporation* (New York: Warner Books, 1985).

12. Weston H. Agor, *Test Your Intuitive Powers: AIM Survey* (Bryn Mawr, PA: Organization Design and Development, 1985).

13. You will note for the purposes of this test I have used the term *thinking* as opposed to *sensing*, which is normally used by other instruments in this field, such as the MBTI. The reason is that during my pretesting, I found that the term *thinking* was clearer to managers than *sensing* to depict analytical and deductive processes.

14. Naisbitt and Aburdene, *Reinventing*, p. 31.

15. Two groups that have been particularly active in generating good quality research are the Mobius Society in Los Angeles, California, and the group of Robert G. Jahn, dean of the School of Engineering at Princeton University in New Jersey. For other work, see Weston H. Agor, *Intuitive Management: Integrating Left and Right Brain Management Skills* (Englewood Cliffs, NJ: Prentice-Hall, 1984).

16. N. R. Kleinfield, "Gentle Persistence Pays Off: Top Headhunters: Lester Korn and Richard Ferry," *New York Times* (October 30, 1983), pp. F6–7. Another similar example was the relationship between Donna Karan and Louis Dell'Olio, the codesigners of the Anne Klein collection since 1974. Judie Glave writes, "At times, she would begin a thought and he would finish it." See "Anne Klein Team Splits Amiably," Associated Press Wire Service (New York), December 20, 1984.

17. Robert J. Cole, "Masters of the Corporate Turnaround," *New York Times* (July 31, 1983), Section 3, p. 1.

18. Martin Lasden, "Intuition: The Voice of Success?" *Computer Decisions* (February 26, 1985), pp. 100–1.

19. See, e.g., Weston H. Agor, "Tomorrow's Intuitive Leaders," *Futurist* (August 1983), pp. 49–53. Also see other related articles such as Arthur J. Levitt, Jr., and Jack Albertine, "The Successful Entrepreneur: A Personality Profile," *Wall Street Journal* (August 29, 1983), p. 12, and Al Siebert, "The Survivor Personality," *Portland Oregonian* (January 27, 1980), p. 3 reprint.

20. For a detailed discussion of opposite types along this and other dimensions, see Isabel Briggs Myers, *Introduction to Type* (Palo Alto, CA: Consulting Psychologists Press, 1980).

21. This treatment on levels of intuitive awareness is discussed in detail in Vaughan, *Awakening Intuition*, pp. 66–80.

22. Tony Bastick, *Intuition: How We Think and Act* (New York: John Wiley & Sons, 1982).

23. Mortimer R. Feinberg and Aaron Levenstein, "How Do You Know When to Rely on Your Intuition?" *Wall Street Journal* (June 21, 1982), p. 16.

24. Jean Shimoda Bolen, *The Tao of Psychology: Synchronicity and the Self* (San Francisco: Harper & Row, 1979), p. 48.

25. Interview Respondent Number 3, 1984–85 Study.

26. Interview Respondent Number 30, 1984–85 Study.

27. Interview Respondent Number 47, 1984–85 Study.

28. Nancy Hathaway, "Intuition: How You Can Recognize It and Make It Work for You," *San Francisco Chronicle* (October 31, 1984), p. cc1.

29. Interview Respondent Number 58, 1984–85 Study.

30. Jonas Salk, *Anatomy of Reality: Merging of Intuition and Reason* (New York: Columbia University Press, 1983), p. 7.

31. Interview Respondent Number 46, 1984 Study.

32. Robert J. Cole, "Telling Pickens That It Won't Be Easy," *New York Times* (November 6, 1983), p. F6.

33. Wayne King, "Trammell Crow Comes to Town," *New York Times* (November 6, 1983), p. F4.

34. Interview Respondent Number 14, 1984–85 Study.

35. See, e.g., "Training Minds to Train Bodies; Redefining Work," *Leading Edge Bulletin* 4, 16 (June 25, 1984), p. 4.

36. See the extroverted intuitive classification of Winston Churchill in William Manchester, *The Last Lion: Winston Spencer Churchill* (New York: Dell Publishing Co., 1984), pp. 18–19.

37. See Isabel Briggs Myers, *The Myers–Briggs Type Indicator: 1985 Manual* (Palo Alto, CA: Consulting Psychologists Press, 1985). This test and other related materials can be obtained from several locations. The two major ones are Consulting Psychologists Press, Inc., 577 College Ave., Palo Alto, CA 94306; and the Center for Applications of Psychological Type, Inc., 2720 NW 6th Street, Suite A, Gainesville, FL 32609.

38. June Singer and Mary Loomis, *The Singer–Loomis Inventory of Personality* (Palo Alto, CA: Consulting Psychologists Press, 1984).

39. For a book that describes this technique, see Charlotte P. Leibel, *Change Your Handwriting, Change Your Life* (New York: Stein & Day, 1972). For a handwriting analyst trained in your area, you may wish to contact the International Graphoanalysis Society, Inc., 111 N. Canal Street, Chicago, IL 60606. If you wish to get a snapshot idea of what this technique can reveal, see Robert W. McLaren, "Handwriting Reveals the Man," *Rotarian* (August 1984), p. 17.

40. Jonas Salk, *Anatomy of Reality*; R. Buckminster Fuller, *Intuition* (San Luis Obispo, CA: Impact Publishers, 1983); and Eric Berne, *Intuition and Ego States* (San Francisco: T.A. Press, 1977) are some examples. For a little more "far out" treatment of one aspect of intuitive ability, consult Dixie Yeterian, *Casebook of a Psychic Detective* (New York: Stein & Day, 1982); Editors of *Psychic*, *Psychics: In-Depth Interviews* (New York: Harper & Row, 1972); and Shawn Robbins, *Ahead of Myself: Confessions of a Professional Psychic* (Englewood Cliffs, NJ: Prentice-Hall, 1980).

41. At a corporate level, a number of organizations every year send their executives on field trips designed to accomplish these objectives. Examples are river rafting and mountain climbing expeditions. Here executives learn more about both their own inherent talents and those of their colleagues as well that they may have ignored up to now.

42. For cassette tapes, see the annotated bibliography sections under the heading "Audio-Visual Materials." One tape that is simply music but no verbal guidance is Steven Halpern and Georgia Kelly, "Ancient Echoes." For verbal guided imagery, you might wish to try either "Develop Your Psychic Abilities" or "Developing Your ESP."

43. See the sections on "Audio-Visual Materials."

44. For details on Alan Vaughan, see his latest book, *The Edge of Tomorrow: How to Foresee and Fulfill Your Future* (New York: Coward, McCann & Geoghegan, 1982).

45. *Success via Synergy* (Fremont, CA: Professional & Organizational Development, 1983).

46. Interview Respondent Number 27, 1984–85 Study.

CHAPTER 5. Implementing a Brain Skill Management Program Within Your Organization

Whether your organization is a computer firm, a major bank, a member of the telecommunications industry, an educational institution, part of the health industry, or a government agency, you have one thing in common: *You wish to survive!* In order to achieve this goal, in all probability you will need to increase your productivity (effectiveness and efficiency) in the future. If survival depends on productivity, it in turn depends on an organization's or individual manager's ability to answer correctly a number of constantly unfolding questions. What will the future look like? What kind of resources (human and physical capital) will be needed to survive in this future scenario? How should they be organized and distributed?

Our ability to answer these questions and then create programs that will effectively implement our response depends in large part on how we organize our human capital resources—personal and organizational. Human capital is potentially the most important resource an organization has for its present and future survival. It is the source for creative solutions to existing problems, and the fountain from which new products and programs will flow. Human capital is also one of the most significant costs in organizational life today. In the public sector, it is usually the major cost item in governmental budgets having the most significant political implications. Yet, even though elaborate personnel and organizational development programs have emerged over the last decade in both the public and the private sectors, the productive use of human capital skills remains a relatively rustic art.

The extensive field research outlined in Part I of this book suggests that you can significantly increase personal and organizational productivity today by immediately implementing a BSM program, which consists of these major components:

- systematic search for and appropriate use of the intuitive talent your organization already has and/or requires;

- systematic integration of this talent with more traditional management approaches to solve critical problems or issues;
- systematic development of the intuitive talent within your organization for applied problem solving;
- creation of a supportive organizational environment in which this program can be implemented.

This chapter outlines how you can implement this new and innovative program. Building on what you have already learned about yourself and your colleagues in Chapter 4, I am going to discuss here in some detail ways you can search for and locate the intuitive talent within your organization; how to productively use this talent to solve critical management problems or issues; steps to take to further develop this intuitive talent for applied problem solving; and finally ways you can take the leadership in creating a supportive organizational environment in which this program can be implemented. Specific examples from actual case studies in both the private and the public sectors will be used throughout the chapter to demonstrate the payoffs to be derived from implementing this program. I will also simulate step-by-step the implementation of one prototype BSM program at a large corporation in the United States (Dow Chemical Company) in order to give you a better sense of what you can expect to occur should you decide to implement such a program within your own organization.

LOCATING AND USING INTUITIVE TALENT

The organization that you work for is probably not much different from most other organizations in America today on one count—up to now, you have not concerned yourself with where the intuitive talent is and whether it exists in sufficient stock to help insure your future survival.

Why look for intuitive talent anyway? What is so special about it? As we discussed in Chapter 4, highly intuitive managers have special skills—skills that are likely to become more valuable in the rapid change environment of the future. They are likely to be the people who will dream up the new products tomorrow that do not exist today. They are the people who can sense whether a new product idea will "fly" in the marketplace successfully. They are the people who "have a feel" for what consumers want and how much they are willing to pay for it. And they are the people who, when asked, will generate the ingenious new solutions to old problems that may have festered for years.[1]

Several of these intuitive managers are names already world famous for their ingenious creativity and/or pioneering inventions: Disney, Land, Salk, and Ibuka.[2] Some are yet unknown. These are the executives that organizations worldwide would dearly love to find. They are the entrapreneurs,[3] the change masters,[4] and the corporate reinventors.[5] They are the executives that Arthur Levitt, Jr., and Jack Albertine describe as having the creative spark, the maverick drive, and the appetite for daring that has served as the catalyst for our economic growth and achievement in this country for more than 200 years.[6]

Let us meet a few of these executive types. One is Chester Carlson, whose invention was turned down by giant businesses that saw no future in his idea. Carlson finally linked up with a small Rochester, New York, company that later grew into one of the nation's major companies, Xerox, thanks to Carlson's invention of xerography.[7] Another is William Smithburg, chairman of Quaker Oats, who encourages his subordinates to take risks in order to grow.[8] Or, take Clive Sinclair, who left school at seventeen to become an inventor. His success as a founder of a personal calculator and computer business is based on the intuitive awareness that you need to create markets in the computer business—not wait for the market to change.[9] Finally, this list of illustrations would not be complete without including the name Estee Lauder, who was famous for having the intuitive instinct of knowing what women wanted in the way of cosmetics.[10]

What should concern you is that *organizations often thwart, block, or drive out this talent*—the very talent they require for their future survival. Or, at the very least, organizations do not have well established human capital management progams designed to search for and consciously use their intuitive talent. As a result, this talent is either not used, suppressed, or often lost altogether. Typically, highly intuitive managers work in an organizational climate that is the opposite of that which enables them to flourish and use their brain skills easily. This climate can be characterized like this. New ideas are not readily encouraged.[11] Higher managers select for staff support other executives who think much like they do rather than emphasizing the fact that they think differently.[12] Unconventional approaches to or methods of solving a problem encounter enormous resistance.[13] It is not long before the intuitive executive begins to emotionally withdraw from the group—slowly but surely reducing his/her input, and often ultimately leaving this organization altogether.[14]

If higher productivity is our goal, clearly we need to create an organizational climate in which intuitive brain skills and styles can flourish and be integrated with other more traditional management techniques. This requires a special sensitivity on the part of the leadership of the organization in question—one that recognizes the special value of intuitive input in decision making and understands how to create an environment in which it will grow.[15] It requires a recognition of the fact that the organization itself will survive in the future only if it makes better use of its existing intuitive talent by integrating it into the mainstream of the organization's regular decision making processes.[16] In short, what is needed is a BSM program in which intuitive talent is consciously searched for, cultivated, and put to applied use.

Let us practice a simulation exercise to see what such a program would consist of and how it might be implemented to increase productivity. As our corporate example, let us take Dow Chemical Company for illustrative purposes.

Dow Chemical Company Simulation*

Let us assume that you are one of the visionary executives who recognize that locating and properly using intuitive talent are important means by which you can increase your organization's productivity. Let us also assume that you are the president of Dow Chemical Company. You know that your company must prepare for a major transition in the 1980s and beyond in order to survive—just as other major organizations in the United States will need to do. Although Dow has had a very successful past performance record as a major supplier of industrial chemicals, you know that market base is quickly changing to one of specialty chemicals and service diversification.[17] The strategy that built the company over the last forty years probably needs to be changed in the near future (see Exhibit 5.1). But what should the new strategy be? How should it be implemented once established? Should the present corporate headquarters continue to be located in Midland, Michigan? Do the top and middle level executives that you presently have on staff match well with future needs? Are they organized properly?

Answers to these and other related strategic questions can be facilitated by the manner in which you proceed to seek solutions to your future direction problem, which we will call the "Dow's Future Project." Let me suggest that besides the traditional methods you would normally employ under these circumstances, you also include as one of your first steps a search for the intuitive talent that you have within Dow (examine the corporate organization chart in Exhibit 5.2). Locating this talent on an individual basis should help you in several ways. First, you probably do not know who your most intuitive executives are, or where they are located in your organization, or how long they have been with the company. Locating this talent will not only get you in touch with this resource, but will also encourage these executives to get in touch with each other on a corporate level in a way never before conceived.

You have just generated a tremendous *potential resource for creative problem solving* that did not exist until now. You may be surprised to find this intuitive talent is located in the most unexpected places (e.g., by division, level of responsibility, and formal role). You may also come to find that this talent has not been as effectively used in the past as it could be in the future (e.g., some intuitive executive talent has been misplaced on the wrong tasks; other intuitive executives are not fully aware of the special talent they possess; and others could benefit from training to strengthen its use). This process may even cause you to change your own traditional concept of what a Dow executive should be like (i.e., useful insights might come from sources you had discounted in the past because their style did not comfortably match yours).

Another important step to take early on in this process is to make clear to this

---

*It should be emphasized that this is only a simulation exercise. Dow Chemical Company has not actually adopted a BSM program as a general management practice to date.

Exhibit 5.1
Events That Require a Change in the Strategic Growth of Dow Chemical Co.

Factors	1942–73	Today and Tomorrow
Raw Materials	Inexpensive, Plentiful	Scarce, Expensive
Capital Requirements	High	Higher
Costs	High Fixed	High Variable
Value Added	High to Medium	Low to Medium
Inflation Rate	Low	High
Interest Rate	Low	High
World Economy	Rapid Growth	Slower Growth
Real Prices	Falling	Rapidly Increasing
Growth Volume	High	Lower

Source: Based on personal interviews with Dow Chemical world headquarters executives in Midland, Michigan, during 1984.

newly established "intuition group" that you recognize and value their talent. Meeting with them personally, giving them a personal charge for action, and indicating that you support the use and development of their talent to help solve Dow's many challenging problems would be a very effective means by which to encourage its actual applied use. Other symbols could also be employed at this stage. Some examples might be running programs and notices on the corporate television channel stressing the importance of intuitive management skills with quotes from you personally indicating that "you recognize their potential value for helping solve Dow's future challenges." Providing funds for the establishment of a corporatewide "intuition club" might be another useful step to take now. Perhaps a third step would be to institute a formal training program at the corporate level where executives could be tested and learn new methods for using and developing their intuitive ability further.

Identifying your highly intuitive executives now may have a number of other useful purposes for Dow as well. For example, research indicates that intuitive executives have a tendency to leave an organization much more quickly when they are dissatisfied than a thinking type is likely to do.[18] Once highly intuitive executives have been identified, it might be useful to assess their satisfaction levels with Dow as a *preventive measure* rather than waiting until the problem

Exhibit 5.2
Dow Corporate Product Management and Planning Assignments, 1984

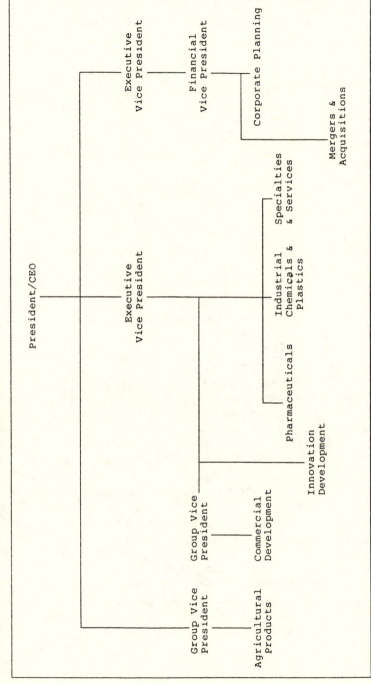

Source: Constructed from personal interviews with Dow
Chemical Co. world headquarters corporate executives
conducted in Midland, Michigan, in 1984.

is too severe to solve. At this point, it might also be worthwhile to assess whether these executives make up a higher percentage among those groups you are making a special effort to recruit in greater numbers to Dow than was the case in the past (e.g., women, blacks). If so, efforts might be initiated now to seek to increase retention rates (e.g., establishment of peer support groups, broader access to outside cultural events). Another step might be to interview these highly intuitive executives to assess whether they feel their ideas have been receiving a receptive hearing within Dow—or systematically discouraged instead. Again, this step could lead to the establishment of new management processes that are likely to increase productivity.

Now that you have located your intuitive talent, there are a number of practical ways you can put it to use to help solve Dow's problems. Let us run through a few examples here to give you a better idea how this process can work. On the "Dow's Future Project," one technique that would be particularly appropriate to use is the Delphi Technique, however, modified in a few important ways from the way it is traditionally run.

Normally, what is done in this approach is to pool expert opinion about what the future will be and make projections based on the common consensus of the experts.[19] However, this technique for projecting the future can be made more accurate with a few key refinements. Your goal in the "Dow's Future Project" is to get an assessment of how some future trends are likely to affect your corporation and to identify ways management should go about dealing with these trends. One way to refine this technique and make it more accurate is to use the BSM assessment instruments discussed in Chapter 4 to identify persons in your organization to be the Delphi projectors. Persons scoring high on instruments that measure intuitive ability (I) would be more likely to be accurate than a random selection of projectors or experts from your major corporate product management and planning assignments listed on the organization chart (see Exhibit 5.2).

One of the instruments we mentioned in Chapter 4 can be used to measure intuitive ability for this purpose. The *AIM Survey* can be used to give you a quick picture of where intuitive talent is located in Dow, the degree to which it is possessed, and whether or not the person appears to be using the skill on the job very effectively. It can also be used to give you an indication of whether the person is presently working in a position where his/her intuitive ability is likely to be used productively. As outlined in Chapter 4, the *AIM Survey* measures on a scale from 0 to 12 intuitive vs. thinking ability. Scores of 10 to 12 would be high on either side of the scale, scores of 6 to 8 would be above average, and 0 to 3 well below average. The instrument also measures whether/how the person tested is actually using his/her intuitive ability on-the-job to make management decisions (see Exhibit 5.3).

If a person is working at his/her full potential, he/she should be *aligned*. That is, the person will be using a style on the job consistent with his/her underlying ability (see Exhibit 5.4). Similarly, for the job to be a good match, it also needs

Exhibit 5.3
Intuitive Management Survey

PART	PURPOSE	STYLE POSSIBLE
I (12 questions from MBTI)	Measures under-lying potential ability	Intuitive (I) Thinking (T)
II (10 questions self-designed)	Measures actual use of ability in decision making	Use (U) Not use (NU) Open (O) Closed (C)
TOTAL AIM Survey	Measures both potential and actual use	I-U, O I-U, C I-NU, C

Exhibit 5.4
***AIM Survey* Scores That Indicate Alignment**

GOOD	Poor
I-U	I-NU
I-O	I-C
I-U+O	I-NU+C

to be aligned. That is, the position should require that the person is using his/her underlying intuitive ability on a regular basis to complete the tasks inherent in that position. Hence, good candidates for the "Dow's Future Project" should score from 10 to 12 on the intuition scale from the *AIM Survey* and should also be those who are most open about using their brain skill and sharing this fact with their colleagues (see Exhibit 5.5).

Let us say that after you have tested key managers across the major Dow corporate product management and planning assignments, you locate thirty peo-

Exhibit 5.5
How to Use Scores on *AIM Survey* for Delphi Project Recruitment

Sample of Potential Candidates							Personnel Action	Reason Selected or Rejected
Number	Score Distribution							
	I	T	U	NU	O	C		
1	10	2	x	–	x	–	Selected	High I, aligned
2	12	0	–	x	–	x	Rejected	High I, but not aligned
3	1	11	–	x	–	x	Rejected	Low I, and not aligned
4	8	4	–	x	–	x	Rejected but subject to training	Good I, but not aligned yet
5	8	4	x	–	–	x	Rejected but subject to training	Good I, but can be more aligned

ple who score from 10 to 12 on the intuition scale of the test, but only ten of these people are properly aligned. These ten managers would be your prime "Dow's Future Project" candidates (examples are cases 1 and 2 in Exhibit 5.5). However, you need not permanently eliminate all the other potential candidates for future projects. The pattern of scores they obtained on the test can be useful information for you to use in the future on this project or to make other changes within your organization that can increase overall productivity.

For example, you may find that some of your potential candidates have very high intuitive ability, but appear to be using a style on the job that is not consistent with it (e.g., candidate 2 in Exhibit 5.5). This manager would appear to be a prime candidate for training programs that would help him/her get better in touch with his/her underlying intuitive ability as well as develop the capacity to rely on this skill to make decisions in a more productive way. At the same time, let us say that a pattern of test scores also suggests that some of your other potential candidates have high intuitive ability, but an analysis of the positions they are currently in indicates that they may well be mismatched. After further analysis and assessment, you may conclude that these managers would be more productive as well as more satisfied personally by reassignment in the organization.

Once you have located and selected your ten highly intuitive managers for this project, there are a number of other techniques you can employ to modify the traditional way of carrying out the Delphi process to make it a still more effective management application for your "Dow's Future Project." Here is how. Remember highly intuitive executives prefer a particular decision making style. They work best when communication is open and informal. The same is true of the work setting—including the way you meet and sit at a table, the clothing you wear, and the color combinations where they normally spend most of their time. They also would prefer to be told to "solve the problem," but bristle at being told *how* to solve it.

Bearing these traits and preferences in mind, how you "organize" the executives selected for your "Dow's Future Project" is critical. You might for example allow the members of the group to decide for themselves how they wish to organize and where/when they wish to meet. If you are not disposed to try this technique, you might select a range of alternatives in between such as alternating between periodic formal and informal meetings. This would also enable you to see for yourself which approach appears to produce the best results. After all, are you not most interested in the product, and not so much how the product team functions to turn it out?

Expert psychologists on the use and development of intuition recommend a number of techniques to help bring this skill "on line" for decision making (see Exhibit 5.6).[20] You might in your charge to this group make clear that they are welcome to try some or all of them, and announce that you are allocating training funds for this purpose should they wish to use both inside or outside resources to assist in the process of learning to use and practice their intuitive skills for application on this project. For example, the group might wish to start their morning meetings with a meditation exercise to help quiet the mind and focus their total energy on the project at hand. "Imagineering" sessions during the day might also be employed, such as asking the group to individually and jointly focus on such key words as "innovation," and then asking, "You are totally free to imagine *new ways* of doing things at Dow—what do you recommend?"

As noted earlier, one of the greatest obstacles to organizational productivity today is bureaucratic regimentation, which has severe repercussions mentally and physically for employees. All too often, routines become established over time which are then hard to alter or eliminate even after their original purpose has long expired. This is particularly true when things appear to be operating smoothly in an organization. The need to change is not at all clearly perceived and blind spots develop. One will often hear in the halls statements like, "But why change—we're doing fine. Besides, we've always done it that way." As a result, it is hard to obtain and maintain a flow of innovative ideas unless there is a crisis present. It is often only then that organizations successful in the past are willing to entertain new ways of doing things in the future. What happens under these conditions? Those executives who are most likely to generate the

Exhibit 5.6
Guidelines to Follow to Develop Your Intuition for Decision Making

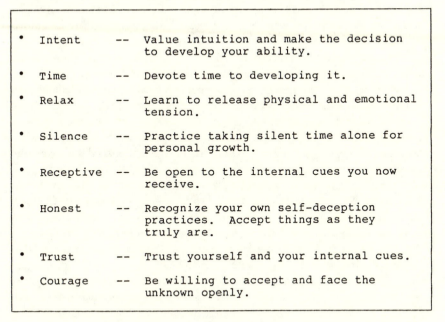

```
•  Intent     --  Value intuition and make the decision
                  to develop your ability.

•  Time       --  Devote time to developing it.

•  Relax      --  Learn to release physical and emotional
                  tension.

•  Silence    --  Practice taking silent time alone for
                  personal growth.

•  Receptive  --  Be open to the internal cues you now
                  receive.

•  Honest     --  Recognize your own self-deception
                  practices.  Accept things as they
                  truly are.

•  Trust      --  Trust yourself and your internal cues.

•  Courage    --  Be willing to accept and face the
                  unknown openly.
```

Source: Developed from a reading of the book by Frances
         E. Vaughan, _Awakening Intuition_ (Garden City, NY:
         Anchor Books, 1979).

greatest number of new and innovative ideas—the highly intuitive executives—
are likely to feel isolated, discouraged, and unappreciated.

When soliciting individual input from the "Dow's Future Project" group,
then, another technique to use which will make the traditional Delphi method
even more effective is the Crawford Slip Method.[21] This is how this technique
works. Whatever particular issue is on the table at the moment, when you are
ready to ask for individual input from which to build the Delphi consensus, hand
out blank slips of paper to the members of the group. You may wish to have
printed on these slips of paper the particular problem being addressed at the
moment to facilitate tabulation later—but that is all. The key point is that the
individual's input should not be identified with that person in any way at all.
The persons should be simply instructed to list on each slip of paper their input
or suggestions or feelings about the issue at hand in clear simple sentences, and
to use as many slips of paper as they need for the ideas they have to offer.

The great advantage of this technique is that it totally facilitates open and free
communication within and from the group. For example, it enables those ex-

ecutives who may not be as effective or willing to express themselves verbally in the group (e.g., introverted intuitives) to have a vehicle where their input (which is often highly valuable) can be gathered rather than potentially lost forever. It also helps to insure that if there is indeed an "expert intuitional consensus," it will be an authentic one—arrived at freely and independently rather than a product of other potential forces such as "group think" or the impact of persuasive personalities (e.g., extroverted intuitives).

Now would be a good time for you to reflect on what you have accomplished by implementing the management approach recommended in the Dow Chemical Company simulation. First of all, you have unleashed and channeled a whole new energy force within your company that has always existed but not productively used before—*intuitive brain skills.* You have accomplished this by getting to know who your highly intuitive executives are and where they are located, and by creating an organizational climate in which their skills can be used most productively. Second, you have also created a communication network that cross-cuts traditional lines of formal responsibility within your organization. In its place, you have established an "energy network" for input to flow based on where the talent is that you need—irrespective of formal roles, sex, or other similar cues. Finally, you have also generated a totally new organizational culture that is conducive to using and developing intuitive brain skills wherever they may exist in the corporation today. As a result, you are more likely to tap into the creative energy that "exists below the water line" that may have escaped your view up to now.

INTEGRATING INTUITION INTO MANAGEMENT DECISION MAKING

Thus far we have talked about the skills and abilities of highly intuitive executives, and emphasized the fact that they have often been overlooked or underutilized in organizations today. At the same time, it is now important to point out that traditional analytical management skills are also certainly an integral and important part of the productive management of organizations today as well as necessary to meet the emerging challenges just ahead. The fact of the matter is that there are particular organizational settings, situations, and circumstances where either intuitive (I) or thinking (T) brain skills are the most appropriate application to use or emphasize (see Exhibit 5.7). Perhaps most important to stress here, however, is that T style managers have certain strengths and weaknesses, that I style managers have certain strengths and weaknesses, and that the most productive organizational culture is one in which the strengths of both are cultivated and integrated into an effective management team effort (see Exhibit 5.8).

For example, on the one hand, thinking style methods and techniques standing alone can lead to faulty conclusions as witnessed by these titles to recent confessionals which appeared in articles concerning erroneous predictions of the stock

Exhibit 5.7
Management Situation Where Brain Style Is Most Appropriate

Level of Application	Two Opposing Brain Styles in Organizations	
	Thinking (T)	Intuitive (I)
Type of organization where predominant	Traditional Pyramid	Open, temporary, or rapid changes
Management style emphasized	Deductive Objective	Inductive Subjective
Example settings where most effective	Quantitative applications where data bases are available	Projection when new trends are emerging Crises Intelligence Holistic health
Example applications	Model building Projection	Brainstorming Challenge traditional assumptions
Occupational specialty	Planning Management Science Financial management Law enforcement and the military	Personnel Counseling Health Organizational development

market: ''Three Errant Seers Tell Where They Went Wrong'' and ''Why Money Managers Bombed.''[22] Similarly, thinking style executives on an individual level have blind spots which can lead to management errors and lost productivity. One example is Joe E. Freeman, Jr., the ex-CEO of AM International, Inc. Although highly regarded for his analytical financial ability and personal integrity, he appeared to lack the intuitive people skills for the job. According to William Givens, one of his colleagues, he failed as a result to generate any staff loyalty, and people simply did not want to work for him any longer.[23]

On the other hand, intuitive executives are not totally free from making errors or mistakes in decision making either. As we saw in Chapters 3 and 4, personal ego factors do at times get in the way of their natural intuitive flow. Very often,

Exhibit 5.8
Combining I and T Type Managers to Best Achieve Organizational Goals

Thinking Managers (T)	Intuitive Managers (I)
• Careful with details. • Strong on followthrough and implementation of programs. • Enjoys handling routine and repetitive tasks. • Works in a smooth fashion day-to-day.	• Good at generating new ideas. • Good creative problem solver. • Can spot new emerging trends effectively. • Can make sense out of situations when data are limited or unavailable.

the intuitive executive who starts a company and provides the charismatic spark of leadership at the outset also fails to institutionalize important good management practices (usually a thinking style manager's forte) which later can lead to the firm's downfall.[24] In the final analysis, what is needed then is the systematic *integration* of intuitive brain skills and styles with more traditional management skills and styles as summarized in Exhibit 5.9. Here is how this can be done.

Return to Dow Chemical Company Simulation

Resuming where we left this exercise, we find ourselves back at Dow Chemical Company. We have already used the *AIM Survey* to test managers for brain skills and styles, and we have also explored ways in which these underlying styles appear to match and not match the job tasks for the positions these executives are now in. But now we also find on further examination that intuitive and thinking managers are often locked in an unproductive struggle resembling the "sudden death overtime" of a Superbowl football game. This struggle is a product of the fact that each management group neither understands nor empathizes with the position and perspective of their opposite brain style types. Rather than trying to work to integrate their respective input into one overall package, each group works feverishly "pounding the other over the head" in an effort to convince them to adopt their respective view on the issue at hand. Neither opposite group fully appreciates how the other thinks and processes.

For example, the legal, engineering, and line production people who tend to be thinking brain types may have difficulty communicating with the marketing and planning personnel who tend to be intuitive brain types. In a typical corporate meeting where both types are present, the intuitive type is quick to see new

Exhibit 5.9
How Different Management Brain Styles Can Combine to Achieve Organizational Goals

Style	Thinking (T)	Intuitive (I)	=	Integrated
Focus	Facts +	Possibilities	=	Facts and possibilities
Methods Used	Practical and impersonal +	Personal, insightful, and enthusiastic	=	Personal, insightful, but also practical
Occupations Where Most Found at Dow	Engineering + Research, Attorneys	Marketing, Planning	=	Effective total organizational team

possibilities or opportunities in a given situation. He/she is quick to generate new ways of overcoming present obstacles. At the same time, the thinking executive's forte is to quickly see the flaws and weaknesses in the new ideas the intuitive type proposes. The net impact is that as soon as new ideas are surfaced by the intuitive types, cold water is thrown on them by the thinking types—often before they have been fully developed or had a fair hearing in the meeting. It is not too long before the intuitive type feels reluctant to surface his/ her innovative proposals for fear of being cut down in an open meeting. Unfortunately, the thinking type manager does not often realize the impact his/her style is having on his/her opposite type. At the same time, this same manager does not normally have the capacity standing alone to generate the new ideas that the corporation needs for its survival that the intuitive type can provide.

This logjam can be overcome and the strengths of each type productively integrated together for the corporation's future well being by taking these steps. Through BSM assessments, you have already taken Step I—selecting your highly intuitive executives for the initial stage of the "Dow's Future Project" (see Exhibit 5.10). Once this group has had a chance to generate their proposals for possible implementation, Step II is to use BSM assessments to select the thinking type managers from the corporate product management and planning staff who are most capable of critically evaluating their suggestion list (this is Step II in Exhibit 5.10). By structuring how these two groups address the same issues in two separate stages rather than simultaneously in the same room at the same time, you have dramatically altered the output of each group separately and the product of the two groups jointly!

What will happen is that the "suggestion list" from Group I (intuitives) will

Exhibit 5.10

How to Use Management Brain Styles to Identify Future Corporate Goals

	STEP I	STEP II	STEP III
Action	Select/assign intuitive group first.	Select/assign thinking group second.	Integrate two groups last.
Capabilities	Sees possibilities. Ingenious. Can deal with complexities and imponderables.	Sees facts. Can analyze organize, and find flaws.	Can identify new ideas that can also be practically implemented. Is conciliatory and persuasive.

start to lengthen and change in content because the "cold water" impact of the immediate criticism from the second group (thinkers) has been removed. At the same time, you have not removed the benefits of analytical critical review from the overall process. This is important to the quality of the final product because we know intuitive managers tend to be careless with facts and detail—especially at the implementation stage of a project. The key change you have made is how this critical review is *structured*. The strengths of each type are emphasized and channeled for productive use while the limitations of each type are reduced or eliminated altogether.

Step III in this process is to finally bring the two separate groups back together to discuss and refine the final product. Again, how this step is carried out is critical. One alternative is to hire an outside consultant to guide this stage. One advantage of doing so is that this person is not likely to be as emotionally involved with the project as the participating staff is. Therefore, he/she should be able to function to ensure greater objectivity and openness to the new concept proposals that are being discussed. Another advantage is to help facilitate the effective interaction between the various brain and management styles in the two groups. This approach is most likely to encourage Group I's creative input since they will feel their input is being truly sought and valued. Similarly, so-called left brain managers will recognize their input is also valued since they will have ample opportunity to review and comment on the proposals that are being surfaced by Group I as well as generate some of their own if appropriate.

There are other techniques that can be used to productively integrate opposite brain styles on the "Dow's Future Project" besides the way the groups are structured to work in the sequence outlined above. One technique is to start training programs whereby key members of your corporate product management and planning group can learn "to see" through the process of actually working on this project that executives with opposite brain skills and styles often offer input that complements their own. All too often, conflict erupts or poor communication develops in an organization largely because two opposite brain types (i.e., thinking vs. intuitive) which also often overlap different occupational specialties (e.g., marketing vs. engineering) come together to work on the same problem with totally different mind sets. Each truly believes they see the world objectively rather than simply a piece of the world in reality. Before long, management focus on solving the problem of the corporation at hand has been displaced by ego conflict over such issues as formal division responsibilities and other personal prerogatives. Until these executives develop a better understanding of how each of their respective approaches is important to the fulfillment of overall Dow goals, conflict will continue and even accelerate.

Training programs can be used to help executives with distinctly different brain styles (including by sex) learn to value and empathize with their opposites to the benefit of the Dow corporation (see Exhibit 5.8–5.10). BSM assessments can be used as a first step to diagnose the pattern of brain and management styles in your overall corporate group as well as by division. Then, key individual executives can be identified who could benefit from more specific follow-up training.

One of the top management executives that I interviewed at Dow for this book is already very sensitive to the value of this technique and the practical input it can have on the quality of management decisions. Through experience, he has found, for example, that the corporate attorneys who report to him have often presented totally thinking style recommendations which are, as he put it, "technically sound but just won't fly in the real world out there." As a result, he encouraged these attorneys to work through a training program of his own where they were taught to learn and practice more intuitive techniques such as, "Think of totally new ways of looking at this problem," or "Have you looked at this problem from all the possible perspectives there are out there vs. just your own?" He states that these attorneys now follow this more integrated pattern of thinking as a regular practice "not only because I'm the boss, but also because *they themselves have seen* that this approach in fact works better."[25]

Let us walk through the steps of how one exercise in such a training program can be used to increase management productivity while actually working on the "Dow's Future Project." This is how I have successfully run this exercise in a number of private and public organizations across the country such as Mountain Bell Telephone Company, Tenneco, the National Security Agency, and the City of Phoenix (see Chapter 6 for more details).[26] Start off with a group of twenty to thirty managers from your corporate product management and planning group who have already been assigned to the "Dow's Future Project." Try to include in this group executives from different management levels and, if at all possible, some managers who are in direct supervisor–subordinate relationships. Also try to include at least two representatives from each sex and to consider other factors such as a wide mix of occupational specialization.

You have already administered the *AIM Survey* test and scored the results before selecting the members of the team. But, the individual members do not yet know how they score or how the other members in the group score. Divide your "Dow's Future Project" group up into two teams. The key now is to load each team by opposite brain type. For our purposes here, let us load the groups so that one team is heavily weighted to the intuitive side of the scale while the other team is heavily weighted in the opposite direction on this same dimension (thinking oriented).

Now the exercise begins. Give each group the same task: "Describe what you think Dow Chemical Company's major goals and products should be by 1990 and through the balance of this century." Ask the members of the group to first write down their own personal response(s) to this question, and then work out a consensus position(s) in each opposite group second—then third in the total project group combined. Provide Crawford slips for the project group to record their respective recommendations at each stage in the exercise. Set a specific time limit for each stage of the exercise, but also make clear that in each stage in the project the individuals and members of each group are free to choose how they will sit and interact.

Throughout the exercise, you periodically eavesdrop on the individual members and the project teams—separately and jointly. Record for playback later such things as how individuals work and process and how individuals and teams interact or fail to interact productively. At the end of the exercise, your role is to interpret the results and share with each participant and group how their *AIM* score affected how they acted and what they recommended for the "Dow's Future Project" at each stage along the way. Since you have kept a detailed record (video taping would also be helpful here), you can now give them live playback about how they interacted.

Here is how you can do this. First of all, discuss and explain the *AIM Survey* and what it measures. Next, explain in a manner that each manager can understand, without being personally exposed, what the results mean. The next step is to explain how and why you loaded the group in the way you did. Here, it might be helpful to reinforce your purpose for doing that, and make clear how this will help to understand how and why they just acted the way they did at each stage of the exercise.

Now the real fun—and real work—begins. Invariably, each team constructed in the manner I outlined will have just worked on the "Dow's Future Project" assignment differently, as will have the individuals in the group. The style they use will normally be different, and the productivity of their work will also vary (as measured by the type, quality, and quantity of the recommendations generated). You can feed back this information to the participants in a variety of ways so that they will clearly know (mentally and emotionally feel) the important practical impact their own brain and management style can have on Dow's and their own productivity and satisfaction.

For example, you can try to explain (and show with video tape playbacks) how each group worked differently. The thinking group tends to break problems down into logical step-by-step chunks and approach the task with a relatively more serious tone. The intuitive group, on the other hand, tends to be lighter in tone and style, and work at the problem in a variety of ways (seldom have I seen intuitives work in order on a project, while thinking types usually do). You can also replay for each individual his/her use of symbolic words, postures, and positions throughout the exercise.

The important point to make all along the way is how the individual and group brain skills and styles affect the project results. Urge the group to focus on such questions as: Were we productive? How could we be more so? Where did we get sidetracked? What did the other group do that we can learn from? Try to move the discussion to both an individual and a group level of awareness at this point. For example, you might take some time now to show how the product of each opposite team was in fact different. Although there was some overlap, in many important ways there was not. This should help sensitize the participants to the importance of listening to their opposite's potential input and hold personal judgment concerning suggestions to the last possible moment. Also, it might be useful here to stress how work styles can be distinct and different—yet both productive. Hence, what is important to learn is what works comfortably for you, and at the same time try to provide sufficient space in your manner of supervision so that opposites can also adopt the organizational style that is comfortable for them too. Finally, you should also stress how the separate teams' lists of recommendations could indeed be combined at Stage III to complement each other and come up with a joint list that was still better than the two separate lists standing alone. It might be helpful now to replay Stage III to drive home and reinforce the integrative skills you have sought to impart here (review Exhibit 5.10).

During this exercise where appropriate—but probably even more effectively later in follow-up sessions—sit down and talk to individual managers while this exercise is fresh in their minds about how their individual brain skills and style affected the overall flow and final product coming from the exercise. You might also spend some time discussing how each person could work more effectively to support each other and the group in the future as you proceed to work on the "Dow's Future Project." This type of personal dialogue is likely to be very sensitive to the persons involved, so try lacing the session with a little humor now and then. This will help them to swallow some sensitive revelations they will probably come to feel along the way. Also remember you have structured the groups to include a few managers who are working "for" each other on a day-to-day basis. Using humor as a vehicle for assisting these executives to internalize what they have just learned can be just the right touch. Example jokes might be "Rise above principle to the politics of the matter," or "You know you are moving in the right direction by the degree to which resistance increases."

What I have tried to demonstrate through this "Dow's Future Project" simulation and exercises is the fact that each brain style and/or personality type has, when standing alone, certain strengths and weaknesses. However, when managers learn to work cooperatively together as a team toward a common goal, blind spots in decision making can be better avoided, productivity increased, and job satisfaction improved enormously by creating an esprit de corps that lifts the spirit to new heights of creativity and imagination.[27] In day-to-day management, what this means is that "we say what we mean and mean what we say." Put another way, future organizational settings will demand that managers not only seek input from their staff, but learn how to use it when they get it. It also means that professional managers and staff need to learn, understand (cognitively and affectively), and value the input received from both intuitive and thinking sources so that it can be integrated into an overall plan of action that is likely to be effective and implementable at the least possible cost. In a nutshell, managers need to learn better how to communicate and be open to communication.

William S. Howell noted in his recent book that the typical CEO makes decisions intuitively and then calls in his/her data person to support the decision analytically.[28] It is clear from what we have presented in this book so far that some managers have outstanding ability to reach the correct (or an effective) decision intuitively. It is also clear that there are situational settings where this approach may be the most effective method to use. But, it is also true that one of the potential dangers for the intuitive manager is projection (incorrectly interpreting one's own wishes to be an accurate perception of reality or the future). One of the best ways to guard against the danger of developing blind spots is to learn to *listen* and *hear* input from other sources, and then integrate this input into the basis for your final decision. It is also one of the best ways of ensuring that you are getting maximum input from your staff as well as yourself. Managers who know (cognitively and affectively) that their input is valued are more likely to give it.

Carl Sagan, the famous author and scientist, puts it this way:

There is no way to tell whether the patterns extracted by the right hemisphere are real or imagined without subjecting them to left-hemisphere scrutiny. On the other hand, mere critical thinking, without creative and intuitive insights, without the search for new patterns, is sterile and doomed. To solve complex problems in changing circumstances requires the activity of both cerebral hemispheres.[29]

Thus far you have learned how to search for intuitive talent in your organization, how highly intuitive managers can be more effectively used and motivated to be more productive, and how this talent can be best teamed with other management types to get management tasks accomplished most productively. Up to now, the primary tool we have used for guiding this process has been the *AIM Survey*. But let us assume for a minute that the project you have in mind requires more precision and in-depth measurement than this instrument can provide. For example, take these management problems which several organizations face today:

* how to productively implement the General Motors Corporation–Toyota Corporation joint venture in California for producing cars;[30]
* how to effectively market your corporate product in Japan;[31]
* how to make the manufacturing and marketing executives at AT&T work productively together.[32]

One test instrument that I introduced you to in Chapter 4 that can be effectively used to help integrate your thinking and intuitive management talent into a combined team effort to address these case problems is the MBTI. Take for example the General Motors Corporation–Toyota Corporation joint venture problem. The key opportunity that appears to exist in this situation is for the management of both companies to learn how to combine the advantages of the intuitive style often emphasized in Japanese management with the deductive and analytical style normally stressed in the United States. When this can be achieved, synergy will become a reality, and productivity as well as job satisfaction will increase dramatically.[33]

There is significant research evidence to indicate that the MBTI can be used effectively to transcend the boundaries of language and culture as in this case to help fashion an integration of brain skills and management styles toward a common end. The Nippon Recruit Center in Tokyo has used a Japanese translation of the MBTI for many years to place workers in business and industry successfully.[34] I also noted in Chapter 2 that my testing of managers nationally indicates that executives with Asian backgrounds on average possess a higher level of intuitive ability that appears to be linked to the way families in the Eastern world bring up their children (inductively) compared to the Western world (deductively). This information along with other test results and personnel data can be used to determine which overall management approach to use in this joint venture case and other similar cross-cultural settings, and to develop the training materials necessary to implement such efforts.[35]

One key difference between the way managers are brought up in this country as compared to Japan and some other countries is in the emphasis on competition vs. cooperation on the job and in our personal lives. There is much evidence to indicate that increasingly managers even in the United States are taking a fresh look at the possible advantages of adopting a more cooperative management style in both the public and the private sectors.[36] This will require a virtual revolution in attitudes—or what is often referred to as a ''quantum leap'' in consciousness. BSM assessment instruments such as the MBTI can be helpful in bringing this change in attitude about successfully. The practical implications for facilitating international cooperation and peace are tremendous.

As was mentioned in Chapter 4, the MBTI can be used not only to identify intuitive managers, but also to identify these managers by particular type if this degree of refinement is practically needed (see Exhibit 5.11). How can this information be used practically? You now have an overall picture of where the brain skills are located in your organization, to what degree, and along separate dimensions. This gives you the necessary tools with the necessary precision to recruit and place your management staff to solve the corporate case problems listed above. For example, if you wish to construct a management team that will not only work well together on a personal basis, but will also possess the brain skills necessary to get organizational problems solved, the MBTI can help in this process.

Exhibit 5.11 outlines how this instrument can be used to search out desired management traits along the full range of available brain skills and preferences, and then integrated together to accomplish organizational goals more productively at the work site. Once managers have been so classified using this instrument, a series of other applications are possible—including designing motivation techniques, assessing turnover rates, guiding internal and outplacement programs, and implementing other programs such as reorganization efforts, mergers, and takeovers.[37]

SYSTEMATIC DEVELOPMENT OF INTUITIVE TALENT FOR APPLIED USE

If highly intuitive executives have special skills that can be used in a variety of management settings, and their talent can be effectively integrated with other brain skills to increase productivity, it is then also desirable for your organization to seek to implement programs that will help develop this talent further for applied use. Below are some management practices for your organization to consider instituting on a regular basis should you decide now to implement a formal program designed to develop further the intuitive talent already existing within your organization.

Recommended here is the implementation of the following management practices that will help to encourage the development of intuitive talent within your organization for applied use:

- Establish an overall organizational model that will facilitate the use and development of intuitive brain skills.

- Structure management teams, groups, and meetings to cultivate and nourish intuitive brain skills consistent with your organizational model.

- Start an "intuition club" within your organization with the specific purpose of developing intuitive brain skills for applied use.

Exhibit 5.11
Using MBTI Scores to Build Management Teams

RANGE OF POSSIBLE INTUITIVE COMBINATIONS			
Type	Skill	Skill	Type
E (Extrovert)	Be able to sell and promote ideas easily.	Be able to sell ideas in small groups or in writing.	I (Introvert)
T (Thinking)	Will express ideas in cool, logical fashion.	Will express ideas in a warm, persuasive manner.	F (Feeling)
J (Judging)	Will work to implement ideas quickly.	Will work to implement ideas in an adaptive fashion.	P (Percep- tive)

Source: Developed from a reading of the book by Isabel
         Briggs Myers and Peter B. Myers, Gifts Differing
         (Palo Alto, CA: Consulting Psychologists Press,
         1980).

New Organizational Model

Implicit in any effort to use and develop intuitive skills is a recognition of the fact that this talent may be (and often is) located throughout your organization at all levels of management and responsibility. In fact, it could well pop up in the most unexpected places and come from persons that may have been previously discounted or shunted aside. Therefore, your organizational management model needs to be sufficiently open, fluid, and flexible to accommodate this reality. Specifically, it means that a highly hierarchical authority structure is probably no longer as functional as it once was. A commitment must be made to asking for and accepting answers from wherever the person is in the organization—not just from department heads or other formal organizational leaders. Leadership will need to be situational, and years of experience with the organization will probably be valued less than in the past. Risk taking and exploring totally new ways of accomplishing your objectives will now be not only entertained but encouraged.

This organizational model is consistent with the recent research findings and experience numerous organizations have had across the country in discovering new ways to increase productivity. For example, in a recent study conducted by McKinsey and Co. of the most successful CEOs nationally, they found that among their key characteristics was a commitment to experimentation—not bureaucracy. They also stress informality rather than a highly structured work environment, and they dare to fix things *before* they break.[38] Similarly, the successful turnaround in Philadelphia of the Great Atlantic and Pacific Tea Co. following greater worker participation and use of existing brain skills demonstrates clearly that a willingness to search for and accept input from all levels of the organization guided by BSM assessments is likely to increase productivity and job satisfaction.[39]

New Management Practices

At the day-to-day level, this means committing yourself and your organization to a mental attitude where innovation is encouraged. It means a willingness to organize groups and meetings in a somewhat less traditional manner, including the acceptance of informal clothing and seating patterns at meetings and the workplace in general and the adoption of more flexible work hours if at all possible.

All too frequently, we reject new and different ways of solving problems because we are simply too accustomed to a particular way of doing things. Often, it is only in a crisis (business failure, change in market) that we are willing to reach for alternative ways of doing things or allow our inherent intuitive skills to surface and be of assistance to us. As Woody Allen says, "If you're not failing every now and again, it's a sign you're not being very innovative in what you're doing."[40] Put another way, making mistakes simply means you are learning faster. It means dropping old management cues such as these if they are not serving any productive purpose: "Follow the rules," "To err is wrong," "That's not my area," or "We've always done it this way."

For example, you may wish to "structure" some of your meetings where the agenda is not formally outlined in great detail. Instead, have a common general purpose for the meeting clearly stated in one sentence, but allow the group to deal with the problem based on the "energy flow" of the participants. Another useful technique is to segment meetings into creative open times to complement structured times. During these open periods, evaluation of proposed ideas (particularly by thinking style managers) is held in abeyance. Experience has shown that this technique is productive because intuitive managers tend to prefer being given a problem to solve, but resent being told how to solve it.[41]

You may also wish to try some of these techniques in place of your more traditional practices. Allow more informal clothing and seating patterns at meetings and the workplace in general. Have music in the background during meetings, including the use of formal meditation exercises before beginning to work on a specific problem. Try this exercise as an example:

Intuitive Meeting Format

• I am going to ask you to relax and sit in a comfortable position.

• Close your eyes now and imagine that you are surrounded by a warm white light.

• Think warmly of the many things you admire and like about your co-workers here. Recall in your mind the many times you have been amazed by their talent. Remember the many times you have been amazed by your own talent.

• Recite softly to yourself, "I have, I am, I can, *I will again today.*"

• Now focus your mind's eye to the problem on the agenda today. Relax, think about it, toss it around in your mind lightly.

• Now, slowly open your eyes at the count of five. When I get to the number five, open your eyes, and feel free to offer what has come to you now. . . .

Instituting practices like these is particularly important for the use and development of the intuitive talent within your organization. Research indicates that highly intuitive executives tend to prefer a very open, flexible management system. They also often prefer a warm environment in which to work—in terms of both colors and interpersonal communication. They appear to function best when they feel their input is truly solicited and given careful consideration. This is particularly so when totally new problems are being addressed where standard operating procedures have not yet been established. Emphasis also on cooperative vs. competitive ways of solving problems appears to generate more productivity from intuitive managers.[42]

Randolph J. Forrester, a city manager in Ohio, has found that establishing an environment where intuition is valued as a management skill has resulted in a number of unexpected and unique solutions to his city's problems. Forrester approaches any given situation with the attitude that he is willing to try anything and a presumption that there is not a 100 percent right way to do anything forever. When a creative idea does not work, he goes back to the old way or tries another approach. This method, Forrester finds, helps employees feel that they are not stuck with a new idea that does not work and yet a positive environment remains in which to keep trying new ideas out. Intuitive thinking, he observes, is not only practical in the sense of being a problem resolution technique, but it is also fun and one of the more psychologically rewarding aspects of management.

To see a new approach or idea become a successful, better way to accomplish something is very satisfying. This approach has worked for me, and has resulted in a number of unique solutions and approaches. These range from women's intern programs and combined meter reader/animal warden positions to self-insured dental/optical/savings accounts.[43]

Another government unit in Nevada has been effectively using and developing its internal intuitive talent by experimenting with a number of the management practices I have mentioned above.[44] The approach they found to be successful was to start with a small group of ten employees initially composed of department and division heads, a first line supervisor, an administrative assistant, a public health nurse, and the assistant county manager. No agenda was set, and no particular methodology was initially adopted on how to go about improving the creativity of the county government.

At first the group began by focusing on developing their own intuitive skills with the eventual goal of transferring what they learned to the governmental units they worked for. There were some false starts and delays, but in the end after two years of work they found they were much more creative than when they started. Through monthly meetings and weekend retreats, the group started working on puzzles found in such materials as Eugene Raudsepp's series of books on creative growth.[45] By working on the puzzles and sharing their solutions, they gained insight into how each group member often blocks creative solutions to problems.

Next, they moved from the puzzles to rigorous brainstorming on hypothetical problems and eventually to actual problems within the county government. They also turned to an outside consultant to assist in the process. Relaxation techniques such as music, art exercises, self-hypnosis, and guided imagery were introduced. They also discussed holistic health and the necessary relationship between mind, body, and spirit. They examined the science or art of knowledge, acupuncture, reflexology, and iridology. They came to realize that to be truly creative required an integration of both thinking and intuitive brain skills.

The group now believes strongly that creativity is a major skill needed to prevent their county from becoming obsolete. They have learned to look beyond traditionally accepted solutions and not to become trapped in the negative power of "group think." Now they also hope to effectively change the total county organization of 1,400 employees by forming separate groups of 10, each led initially by members of the original team.

Another significant management practice you may wish to consider implementing in your organization is an organization development/transformation program that helps to insure that management staff are exposed early in their career to a variety of tasks and situations that encourage the use and development of their intuitive skills. Research suggests that breadth as well as depth of management and related life experiences are conducive to developing intuitive skills.[46] So too are regular rotational experiences to help ensure that organizational routines do not become so ingrained that one loses the ability to think up or create better ways of doing things. Put another way, care needs to be taken to ensure that thirty years of experience "does not mean having the same experience thirty times."

One highly successful organization, Procter & Gamble, practices in effect elements of such a program when they develop promising new marketing executives. All prospects on this career path are required to work in a field sales position for the first six months to learn to understand first hand the problems one faces on the firing line. The philosophy is that this experience will better enable the prospect to later devise marketing programs in the main office that can realistically be implemented in the field. After this period, a prospect is moved to a line marketing position in brand management. A practice of lateral rotation from brand to brand at regular intervals is followed after that to broaden the person's management and product experience. This practice does help to maintain a creative mind set among the marketing staff. However, even this successful company could be significantly more so if they went further to implement the other practices outlined above.[47]

Establish an Intuition Club

A third way to encourage the development of intuitive brain skills in your organization is to start a formal "intuition club" at work. At this point in most organizations in America, this step is necessary in order not only to emphasize the inherent value of using intuitive management techniques, but also to re-establish a more integrated balance to our present practices which tend to over-emphasize more traditional management techniques. As a general rule, the typical organization today already provides a variety of opportunities for developing traditional management skills such as computer workshops and accounting clinics. But little formally or informally exists to help train and develop intuitive skills in the same manner for applied use.

One innovative use of this club concept serves to demonstrate how this technique can be practically used within your organization for similar purposes. Inferential Focus, a firm located in New York City, specializes in using intuitive techniques to predict future trends for blue chip clients. In an effort to help themselves stay current on "the state of the art" in this field as well as helping in the process of developing new cutting edge applications themselves, they have established an advisory "right brain club" which is nationally based for this purpose. New methodology, approaches, articles, and related information are exchanged among the members through a regular mailing, and each member is encouraged to provide his/her own input whatever it is. This club also serves to provide emotional support and encouragement among members as they engage in the process of developing their own intuitive skills further.[48]

The establishment of an "intuition club" within your organization should have as its primary purpose the demonstration of the fact that the use and development of intuitive skills will increase productivity and job satisfaction. At the outset, it is recommended that membership be confined to those executives with the highest intuition scores on the *AIM Survey* (i.e., 10 to 12), but open at the same time to any employee who scores in this range irrespective of his/her formal position in the organization. This will enable you to locate your best intuitive talent and establish a clear track record of success. Once this has been accomplished, membership can be broadened later to include anyone who wishes to work on using and developing his/her intuitive skills.

It might be useful to establish an internal newsletter for facilitating communication within the group, for maintaining interest, and perhaps for networking with other similar clubs in other organizations. This process could be accomplished in part through a modern computer data bank system as well where persons could log in and off the system as convenient based on their work schedule and personal style. You might even wish to explore the feasibility of extending your club's network beyond your own organization. For example, as in the Inferential Focus example noted above, you might find it to your advantage to exchange with other similar clubs or individuals on a regional, national, or even international basis (the appendix of this book provides further details on how this can be accomplished if you wish to do so).

SUMMARY

You have seen in this chapter how a BSM program can potentially be used to increase productivity and job satisfaction within your organization. Specifically, you have learned how to search for intuitive brain skills and integrate them with more traditional management techniques normally practiced today to solve critical problems or issues. You have also learned how to implement a BSM program that will help you to use and develop the intuitive talent already existing within your organization more effectively. Here, we have recommended instituting a series of new organizational and management practices and the establishment of an "intuition club."

Turn now to Chapter 6 where you will see how some of these recommended techniques have actually been used to increase productivity in both private and public sector organizations. Two individual case studies will be described in some detail to illustrate for you the potential BSM has, and also to give you a greater understanding of how intuitive brain skills in particular can be used in this regard.

NOTES

1. For many illustrations of this ability, see Karl Albrecht, *Brain Power: Learn to Improve Your Thinking Skills* (Englewood Cliffs, NJ: Prentice-Hall, 1980).

2. "Innovation That Crosses Cultural Lines," *New York Times* (January 22, 1984), p. F17.

3. Gifford Pinchot III, *Entrapreneuring* (New York: Harper & Row, 1984).

4. Rosabeth Moss Kanter, *The Change Masters: Innovation for Productivity in the American Corporation* (New York: Simon & Schuster, 1983).

5. John Naisbitt and Patricia Aburdene, *Reinventing the Corporation* (New York: Warner Books, 1985).

6. Arthur J. Levitt, Jr., and Jack Albertine, "The Successful Entrepreneur: A Personality Profile," *Wall Street Journal* (August 29, 1983), p. 12.

7. "Inventive Genius Is Alive and Well in the U.S.," *U.S. News and World Report* (June 13, 1983), p. 61.

8. Sue Shellenbarger, "Quaker Oats Chairman to Continue to Make Changes in New Position," *Wall Street Journal* (November 11, 1984), p. 25.

9. Jeffrey Robinson, "Blooming Genius: Inventor Clive Sinclair Strikes It Rich," *Barron's* (December 12, 1983), p. 14.

10. Gigi Mahon, "Sweet Smell of Success: Meet Cosmetic Executive Lindsay Owen-Jones," *Barron's* (December 5, 1983), p. 30.

11. For example, inventor Clive Sinclair established his own computer company because he noted that older companies found it very hard to innovate once they had established their own way of doing things. See Robinson, "Blooming Genius," p. 36.

12. This example is repeated over and over in organizations. One product of this closed, non-competitive bureaucracy is the Central Intelligence Agency's failure to correctly estimate Soviet arms spending. For details, see Lev Navrozov, "Why the CIA Undershoots Soviet Arms Spending," *Wall Street Journal* (December 6, 1983), p. 28.

13. Dr. Gerald Holton, a science historian at Harvard University, warns that all too often good intuitive ideas are thwarted by the establishment clinging with white knuckles to the familiar theories of the past. Holton points out numerous situations where a person has a good idea, but encounters enormous problems if he/she works outside the normal framework. See William J. Broad, "The Science Corps Wants a Few More Good Heretics," *New York Times* (October 16, 1983), p. EY8.

14. Research indicates that highly intuitive executives are more likely to leave the organization than thinking types under these circumstances. See Isabel Briggs Myers and Peter B. Myers, *Gifts Differing* (Palo Alto, CA: Consulting Psychologists Press, 1980).

15. For a detailed discussion concerning how to create this organization climate, see Weston H. Agor, *Intuitive Management: Integrating Left and Right Brain Management Skills* (Englewood Cliffs, NJ: Prentice-Hall, 1984).

16. See Naisbitt and Aburdene, *Reinventing*.

17. See *The Dow Chemical Company: 1983 Annual Report* (Midland, MI: Dow Chemical, 1984).

18. Myers and Myers, *Gifts Differing*.

19. For a discussion of this technique, see William Ascher, *Forecasting: An Appraisal for Policy-Makers and Planners* (Baltimore: Johns Hopkins University Press, 1978), p. 184.

20. Perhaps the leading psychologist in this country on the subject of intuition is Frances E. Vaughan. See her *Awakening Intuition* (Garden City, NY: Anchor Books, 1979).

21. C. C. Crawford and John W. Demidovich, "Think Tank Technology for Systems Management," *Journal of Systems Management* (November 1981), pp. 22–25.

22. Floyd Norris, "Bear with Us: Three Errant Seers Tell Where They Went Wrong," *Barron's* (February 13, 1984), pp. 8–9; Anise C. Wallace, "Why Money Managers Bombed," *New York Times* (January 22, 1984), p. F4.

23. Meg Cox, "Ex-Chief of Recovering AM International Appears to Be a Victim of His Own Success," *Wall Street Journal* (January 27, 1984), p. 25.

24. For a discussion of the importance of integrating so-called left and right brain management skills to avoid this type of pitfall, see David Loye, *The Sphinx and the Rainbow: Brain, Mind and Future Vision* (Boulder, CO: Shambhala, 1983).

25. Interview Respondent Number 14, 1984–85 Study.

26. Each of these organizations is going through megatrend changes at this time, which make BSM programs particularly useful. Searching out intuitive brain skill talent to

address the problems brought about by these changes is a particularly productive application of BSM programs.

27. See Sharon L. Connelly, "Work Spirit: Channeling Energy for High Performance," *Training and Development Journal* (May 1985), pp. 10–15.

28. William S. Howell, *The Empathic Communicator* (Belmont, CA: Wadsworth Publishing Co., 1982), p. 231.

29. Carl Sagan, *The Dragons of Eden* (New York: Random House, 1977), p. 181.

30. John Koten, "GM–Toyota Venture Stirs Major Antitrust and Labor Problems," *Wall Street Journal* (June 10, 1983), p. 1.

31. Heywood Klein, "Firms Seek Aid in Deciphering Japan's Culture," *Wall Street Journal* (September 1, 1983), p. 1.

32. Monica Langley, "AT&T Marketing Men Find Their Star Fails to Ascend as Expected," *Wall Street Journal* (February 13, 1984), p. 1.

33. For details on how this can be done, see Agor, *Intuitive Management*, Chapter 3.

34. Myers and Myers, *Gifts Differing*, p. 208.

35. For an outline of how, see Weston H. Agor, "Using Brain Skill Assessments to Increase Productivity in Development Administration," *Public Administration and Development* 4, 4 (October–December 1984), pp. 335–42.

36. See, e.g., William Serrin, "Companies Widen Worker Role in Decisions," *New York Times* (January 15, 1984), p. 1.

37. For more details, see Weston H. Agor, *Test Your Intuitive Powers: AIM Survey* (Bryn Mawr, PA: Organization Design and Development, 1985), pp. 11–12.

38. Arthur J. Levitt, Jr., and Jack Albertine, "The Successful Entrepreneur: A Personality Profile," *Wall Street Journal* (August 29, 1983), p. 12.

39. Paul A. Engelmayer, "Worker Owned and Operated Supermarket Yields Financial Success, Personal Rewards," *Wall Street Journal* (August 18, 1983), p. 23.

40. Cited in Roy Rowan, *The Intuitive Manager* (Boston: Little, Brown, 1986).

41. See Weston H. Agor, "Brain Skill Development in Management Training," *Training and Development* 37, no. 4 (April 1983), pp. 78–83.

42. See, e.g., Philip Goldberg, *The Intuitive Edge: Understanding and Developing Intuition* (Los Angeles: J. P. Tarcher, 1983).

43. Cited in Commentary Section of *Public Management* 65, 2 (February 1983), p. 17.

44. Ed Everett, "Improving Creativity—One Organization's Approach," *Public Management* 65, 2 (February 1983), p. 7.

45. Eugene Raudsepp with George P. Hough, Jr., *Creative Growth Games* (New York: Perigee Books, 1977); Eugene Raudsepp, *More Creative Growth Games* (New York: Perigee Books, 1980); and Eugene Raudsepp, *How Creative Are You?* (New York: Perigee Books, 1981).

46. See Thomas J. Peters and Robert H. Waterman, Jr., *In Search of Excellence: Lessons from America's Best-Run Companies* (New York: Warner Books, 1983).

47. I speak from personal experience, having once been employed by Procter & Gamble in the international division, advertising brand management for several years.

48. "The Right Brain Club: Advisory Network of Inferential Focus" (New York: Inferential Focus). I am a member of this national network.

CHAPTER 6. How to Use Intuitive Decision Making to Increase Productivity: Case Study Illustrations

In the last two chapters, you have learned a good deal about how to use and develop your intuitive ability to increase productivity—both at an individual and at an organizational level. You have also learned steps to take in order to systematically integrate this ability with more traditional management skills on a day-to-day basis toward the same end. This chapter will give you an even greater understanding of how intuitive decision making skills can be used to increase productivity through the description of two case studies where such programs have actually been tried successfully.

One case illustration is from the private sector (Tenneco, Inc.) and one is from the public sector (the City of Phoenix). These two specific cases were selected for several reasons. Both organizations are large in size and have complicated structures to manage. They both regularly must face and learn to deal with the types of problems most conducive to intuitive decision making (e.g., crises, rapid change, and new emerging trends). If intuition can be a useful management skill, it should be readily demonstrable in these organizational settings. Finally, these cases were selected because I had been asked by each organization to conduct a workshop on intuitive decision making for either their upper level management or professional staff. The problems in each case selected for illustration here were ones we worked on in these workshops. Therefore, detailed data on how intuitive skills can be used and developed for problem solving were readily available for analysis. It should be noted, however, that the two case studies and problem solving examples selected here for description are very typical of those encountered in a wide variety of other private and public sector organizations where I have consulted.[1] Therefore, what is said here is probably applicable to your own organizational setting as well.

THE TENNECO, INC., CASE

Tenneco is a large, diversified, energy based company which ranks sixteenth largest in net income and nineteenth in sales on the *Fortune* 500 listing of major

United States industrial corporations. Since the company's birth in 1943, net income and assets have doubled nearly every five years. As a result, Tenneco is one of the youngest corporations among *Fortune's* top twenty companies.[2]

Faced with a highly cyclical environment in the energy side of the business, Tenneco has embarked on a long-term strategy of diversification through the acquisition and development of non-energy subsidiaries.[3] Simultaneously, a concerted effort is underway throughout the company to apply the latest available technology to increase quality and productivity—including the "state of the art" knowledge on BSM. One component of this overall program is the Staff Professional Program. Tenneco recognizes that staff professionals need to learn to adapt to an ever increasing rate of organizational change as they seek to meet competitive pressures at home and abroad. Accordingly, the Staff Professional Program is designed to provide their professional staff with the personal and technical skills necessary to function effectively.[4] One element of this program includes training in how to be a catalyst for innovation through the learning of creative thinking and problem solving skills.

In October 1985, forty-five professional staff members from around the country were assembled in a corporate retreat site outside of Tenneco's Houston corporate headquarters called Columbia Lakes to take part in this program. My particular charge was to teach and demonstrate in one day's time how intuitive brain skills could be used by this group to stimulate innovation.

The workshop was organized following basically the same steps you have gone through in this book (see Exhibit 6.1 for a detailed outline of the workshop).[5] First, the latest research findings and perspectives on brain research were presented so that the participants could become acquainted with "the state of the art" to date, and gain a sense of the quantum leaps in our understanding about how the brain functions which are just around the corner in this next decade. Second, participants were tested and given immediate feedback on their brain skills and styles using the instruments discussed in Chapter 4—both on an individual and on a group basis. Next, participants were shown how the BSM assessments could be practically used to engineer change in a variety of ways. Particular emphasis was placed on the role of intuitive skills in this regard. Then, the group was taught through a series of "hands-on" exercises how the BSM assessment just completed could be used in a variety of ways to increase productivity—again with emphasis on the role of intuitive brain skills in the process. A feature of this part of the workshop was extensive work on a real Tenneco problem that a division of the company wanted to address called "Tenneco Ventures," which was guided by the BSM assessment just completed (more on this later). Finally, the workshop was concluded with an introduction to techniques that the staff professionals could practice on their own and/or in a group later to develop their intuitive skills further for applied use.

Here are the highlights of how this process in fact worked. Participants were each given a workbook at the beginning of the workshop that contained the outline, the *AIM Survey* and scoring instrument, and several charts and tables

Exhibit 6.1
Outline of Intuitive Management Workshop at Tenneco

```
Introduction--Management Climate of the Future

Latest Research Findings and Views

Brain Skill Testing and Assessment

How to Practically Use BSM Assessments to Engineer
Change

How to Use Intuitive Brain Skills to Increase
Productivity at Tenneco

   * Find creative talent irrespective of position or
     title.

   * Match to particular problem/situation.

   * Team building.

   * Recruitment and placement.

   * Guard against blind spots in own decision making.

   * Guide for the design of future training programs.

Work on the "Tenneco Ventures" Project

Expand Your Intuitive Brain Skills:  The Challenge

   * Steps to take.

   * Exercises to practice.

   * Hands-on practice.

   * Resources to conduct for the future.
```

that summarized the main points of the presentation that day. At the outset, I briefly reviewed the materials contained in the workbook so that the participants knew they could later concentrate their attention on my presentation itself since many of the main points were already summarized in the hand-out materials. In addition, I gave each participant a number. The purpose of doing this was so that we could later share individual test scores in the group without anyone other than the participant himself/herself knowing exactly who the individual scores corresponded to.

After the test was completed and scored, individual scores were collected by assigned number as described above, and then tabulated to obtain the total group score, the score by sex, and also the score by brain skill type. This provided me with the data to immediately feed back to the participants how they scored not only individually but also by sex, compared to the total Tenneco group and also compared to the national norms discussed in Chapter 2.

This information was immediately displayed on an overlay projector so each individual and the group as a whole could easily follow my discussion concerning the results and how to use them in a practical way to increase productivity at Tenneco. In addition, each participant workbook had a score sheet like that on the overlay so they could record scores themselves and make notes on how to interpret and use the findings in a practical way.

Exhibit 6.2 displays for you some of the scores for a selected sample of the participants in the group. You will also see mean scores for all the men and women in the Tenneco group, and the mean scores for all forty-five participants as compared to national norms (see Exhibit 6.2). Displaying this information immediately back to participants in this way has a number of advantages. Individuals can see how they score compared to their colleagues and national norms, but in a way that does not violate confidentiality. They can also see instantaneously how the scores vary within the group quite significantly, which can later be used to demonstrate how to build problem solving teams that will work more productively. Finally, they can also see how the Tenneco group as a whole compares to national norms, which can later be used to illustrate how this group of staff professionals will tend to approach and try to solve a particular problem.

As you can see in Exhibit 6.2, men scored lower than women on intuitive ability, which is consistent with national norms. But, it is equally important to note that both sexes in the Tenneco group score below the national average on intuitive ability as does the total group. Compared to the national sample, the Tenneco group can be said to be somewhat more thinking (analytical, deductive) in brain skill and style than the national sample. Within the Tenneco group, however, individual scores vary quite significantly for both sexes. What is important to do now is to assess whether these individuals are well aligned (i.e., if they are working in jobs that make the best use of their particular brain skill and style). From a strategic planning perspective, the question can also be legitimately asked whether Tenneco is presently attracting to the organization the brain skills most appropriate to meet the challenges the megatrend environment is now starting to generate for the company.[6]

As noted in Chapter 5, these brain skill scores can also be used in a number of different ways to help participants achieve a better cognitive understanding of their own brain skills and abilities and the brain style they use to try to solve a particular problem at work. For example, in this Tenneco group, numbers 2, 11, and 15 are likely to practice thinking styles of decision making, and probably would find that working together in a problem solving group would be a relatively easy task to do. On the opposite end of the scale, numbers 6, 7, 20, and 29 would probably practice intuitive styles of decision making. They too would probably function easily as one problem solving group. Each respective group has certain strengths and limitations, however, and so how they are sequenced

Exhibit 6.2
Brain Skill Scores for Tenneco Staff Professionals

Selected Sample of Participants		Score	
Number	Sex	Intuition	Thinking
2	FM	3	9
6	M	12	0
7	FM	9	3
11	FM	0	12
15	M	2	10
20	M	11	1
21	M	7	5
26	M	6	6
29	FM	10	2
Total Scores (Complete Sample)			
Mean for Tenneco Men		5.4	6.6
Mean for National Men		6.3	5.7
Mean for Tenneco Women		6.1	5.9
Mean for National Women		6.9	5.1
Mean for Tenneco Group		5.2	6.8
Mean for National Sample		6.4	5.6

together could dramatically affect group productivity (see Chapter 5). You will note number 26 has a tied score of 6 and 6. This person often is pulled in two different directions by factual cues on the one hand and feeling cues on the other. It is not uncommon for this person to have great difficulty making a final decision and often to experience a great deal of tension in the process. As a result, frequently this person will unnecessarily delay a decision and/or tend to over-analyze a problem before finally acting.[7]

One of the most productive aspects of reviewing these score results with participants is that they often serve as a vehicle by which individuals can learn to deal with and feel more comfortable with their own particular style. This may mean, for example, that you have the right person in the wrong position or working in the wrong group setting. Or it may mean that hearing about their brain skills and styles touches a chord inside that really tells them what they already know to be true, which can later serve as a catalyst for action (e.g., seek a job change, go for personal counseling). Very often, participants share more comfortably this type of personal information during the break periods. This is often when the most productive work is really done because participants feel much more comfortable one-on-one sharing in confidence what they have learned or asking questions the discussion may have prompted.[8]

As outlined in Exhibit 6.1, there are a number of ways brain skill scores can also be used to make the best use of the intuitive talent already existing within your organization to help increase productivity. One way is to first of all identify your intuitive talent. As noted in Chapter 5, all too often organizations do not know how much intuitive talent they have and where it is located. As a rule, we are more likely to know our staff instead in terms of formal job title or years of experience. Of the forty-five participants in the Tenneco group, only twelve were dominant intuitive. Within this subgroup, seven of the twelve scored in the high intuitive range (10 to 12 on the *AIM Survey* scale). This subgroup— especially the high intuitives—is probably the best human capital resource within the Tenneco group to consult when you need new ideas, problem solving solutions, or other creative input. It is also important to note that four of the seven in the group of highly intuitives are women. It would be important to assess how this subgroup is presently being used at Tenneco (i.e., what occupations, tasks, and level of responsibility). Identification of intuitive talent and assessing how it is presently being used could well suggest a number of specific ways productivity could be increased.[9]

Another way to use these intuitive scores is to help establish an internal network by which this talent can be more effectively used and developed. Just as it is usually true that organizations do not know who their intuitive talent is, it is also often true that intuitive executives do not know each other either. As a rule, no formal organizational mechanism exists to identify and channel this talent for applied use. Furthermore, as we noted in Chapter 3, highly intuitive executives tend to keep it a secret that they use this skill to guide their process of decision making.[10]

The technique I use to introduce intuitives to each other for the first time is to put them together on a problem solving exercise the organization would like to solve. This has several advantages. First, these intuitive executives get to meet each other in a formal way guided by brain skill testing. Second, by working on a real problem solving exercise, they get to demonstrate to the entire workshop group (and themselves) their skills and abilities. Finally, when the results are presented to the whole group for all to see, it serves to encourage everyone to think about the intuitive ability they may have within that can be used in an applied way more effectively.

At Tenneco, this was accomplished as follows. The staff professionals were divided into smaller working groups guided by the brain skill testing just completed. Care was taken to be sure one work group was composed only of the highly intuitive executives. A "Tenneco Ventures" problem was selected to work on. Tenneco Ventures, Inc., is a wholly owned subsidiary of Tenneco formed in August 1984 with the mission of defining high growth areas for investment. The company has particular interest in concentrating on areas where Tenneco has a competitive advantage (e.g., superior ability to evaluate technology for the exploration and production of oil and gas; market knowledge through computer aided design of new products; diversity of expertise and knowledge to draw on throughout the company). Current areas of particular interest are

- factory automation;
- resource technology;
- bio-technology;
- computer applications such as software and information management systems.

Tenneco Ventures is looking for good investment ideas where they can provide the capital to help establish new businesses or revitalize existing ones. Another objective is to provide an incentive for innovative entrepreneurs to remain with the company to help develop an atmosphere within that will encourage new ideas.[11] For the workshop purposes, I sought to demonstrate that the intuitive group would produce the longest and best list of ideas for potential investment. I also wished to demonstrate to each subgroup that the list of ideas they produced often did not match those of the other subgroups, and this fact was linked to their "going in brain skill and style." Finally, I also wished to demonstrate to the whole Tenneco group how productivity could be increased by the manner in which brain skill/style groups were sequenced in the problem solving exercise at hand.

The Crawford Slip Technique discussed in Chapter 5 was used to help facilitate the free flow of ideas in each group. Once the exercise was explained, slips were handed out to each participant in the various subgroups. Each participant was instructed to write down on each slip as many ideas as he/she could think of that met the Tenneco Ventures criteria. Once this step was completed, all the slips in each subgroup were handed to a subgroup facilitator also selected on the basis of brain skill scores. They were instructed to first of all simply record each and every suggestion on a flip chart provided without comment or criticism by the subgroup. Once this was done, each subgroup was instructed to discuss the total "list of ideas" presented there, and agree on a group of four or five that they would like to recommend to the total staff professional group. In the meantime, I moved from subgroup to subgroup recording notes about how each proceeded to work on this problem for playback later.

The product of this exercise functioned as planned. First of all, the highly intuitive table of executives did come up with the longest and best list of suggestions as agreed to later by the vast majority of the participants. However, it is also important to note that several of their ideas were also not very realistic—a fact pointed out later by the thinking tables of executives who are most likely to be able to critically evaluate the new ideas of others before implementation. It is also important to note that each subgroup table approached the problem and dealt with it in a highly predictable manner based on brain scores. For example, the highly intuitive table did not sequentially review the list of ideas presented as the thinking tables did. Instead, they tended to bounce around from front to back, to the middle of the list—almost at random. They also tended to adopt a more playful style toward solving the problem, often bursting out in loud laughter, whereas the T tables tended instead to be quite serious about working on the task, worked in a very methodological fashion, and often checked their watch to be very sure they finished on time. Finally, when each subgroup reached the point of trying to achieve a consensus on their final recommended list, the intuitive table almost reached the decision by what might be called "feel" whereas the thinking tables tended to decide by a tabulation of hands or votes with the majority ruling.

When each subgroup presented their "final recommended list" to the total Tenneco group, the vast majority of suggestions agreed to at each table did not overlap. The importance of this finding is that it demonstrates very clearly the fact that how groups are structured to work on an organization problem by dominant brain skill dramatically affects the total output of the group. Here is why this is so. By their very nature, highly intuitive managers tend to be more open to new and different ways of doing things. They also get more enjoyment from solving an ever new list of problems rather than working with a similar problem time after time. They tend by personality type to be somewhat more flexible in their work style and, as a general rule, more open to the opposing ideas of others. Hence, their subgroup list of venture ideas tends to be better and larger. On the other hand, the thinking groups tend to be much better at criticizing and evaluating new ideas vs. generating new ideas of their own. They also tend to "see or be conscious of" a more limited number of new but potentially plausible options for solving a problem at hand. Therefore, as a group they are more likely to also be prone to "group think," which is the process by which new ideas are offered only if they fall within the range considered by the group as acceptable, often resulting in very plausible ideas never being surfaced in the group.[12]

For these reasons, the quality and quantity of output will be dramatically increased in organizations if groups are formed first guided by brain skill assessments, and then sequenced so that each brain skill type is put on the problem at the stage in the process where their skill is most appropriate. In the "Tenneco Ventures" exercise, the best group to generate new ideas is the intuitive group—especially the high intuitives. It is recommended therefore that they be first given the task of generating "the new venture ideas," and that they work in subgroups totally apart from the thinking subgroups. Second, it is then recommended that this list of ideas be evaluated by the thinking subgroups. They are best at critically evaluating the input of others—particularly as it relates to the feasibility of a proposed idea at the implementation stage. Finally, it is recommended that these two "opposite type" subgroups then be brought together as a third step to further refine and assess the project ideas recommended. Often at this stage, a few additional new ideas will be generated by this type of interaction that can also be added to the list (review Chapter 5 again for a more detailed discussion of this process).

Exhibit 6.3 summarizes some of the very best ideas generated in the "Tenneco Ventures" project using all of the techniques outlined above:

• work groups formed first and foremost guided by brain skill and style assessments;
• work groups sequenced to match the stage in the process where each brain skill functions most effectively;
• use of the Crawford Slip Technique to help facilitate open intuitive communication and input at each stage in the process.

Once the whole Tenneco group became more sensitive to the capabilities of the intuitive talent existing in the group and also how this brain skill could be systematically integrated with analytical brain skills that also existed, I proceeded to discuss other potential applications of a BSM program in some detail. For example, as noted in Chapter 5, such assessments can be used as one means to help guide future recruitment programs once it is clear from the process what type and mix of brain skills you presently have, as compared to what you appear to need in the future. They can also be used to assess communication problems within an organization and work effectively to help resolve them. Finally, a BSM program can be used to help guide the design and implementation of a corporate or public sector training program. For example, managers desiring or requiring more complete thinking skill development (deductive reasoning and analytical ability) could be channeled to particular courses, workshops, or clinics where this would take place. For managers seeking to learn how to develop their intuitive skills and to apply them to solving real problems they face in organizational settings, these executives could be similarly channeled to programs where these skills could be more fully developed and actualized.

One of the most exciting and productive parts of this case study workshop was helping participants learn about their intuitive brain skills and how to develop them further. Here a selected sampling of the techniques outlined in Chapters 4 and 5 was used as time allowed. For example, participants were introduced to the practice of meditation—many for the first time in their life. For this group, it was both exciting and also a time of some "apprehension" because many members were entering a field they had not tried before. Selected samples of different meditation exercises and tapes were used (e.g., breathing and relaxation techniques; guided and not guided imagery tapes) so that each participant could get some feel for the existing resources that might be consulted later. Also, it gave participants a chance to get a sense of how they themselves responded to each particular technique.

Participants were also introduced to several other techniques for developing their intuitive ability such as "keeping an intuition journal," establishing an "intuition club or network" within Tenneco, and steps to follow in working to

Exhibit 6.3
Sample Tenneco Ventures Projects Produced Guided by Brain Skill Assessments Exercise

---

* Develop an ultrasonic continuous inspection system for materials such as paper, metals, glass fabrics, and some plastics.

* Develop laser well drilling.

* Develop jet cutters.

* Develop non-frictional drilling process.

* Develop a disposal system for oilfield waste which is environmentally safe.

* Develop an aquaculture water purification system.

* Form a Tenneco computer company.

* Develop a line of retail products which offer a completely balanced meal package.

* Develop a more efficient solar collection system.

---

enhance their ability—both alone and in a group. As a rule, for most of the professionals in this group, this was all totally new information to them. The intuitive subgroup on the one hand instinctively took to the subject at this stage of the workshop, and tended to easily fall into such exercises as "create your own mental workshop." The thinking group, however, tended to have more difficulty with this portion of the day. The reasons are clearly related to their own brain style and personality. Exercises at this stage often require "leaps of faith" leaving behind the security blanket of "facts" that this subgroup normally relies on to guide most of their actions. Often here participants are faced with arriving at a totally new awareness of what reality is without being able to understand or explain step-by-step how they arrived at this point.

At this stage in the workshop, courage is also often required to face one's own self as one really is and to some degree the unknown this process implies lies just ahead as one proceeds on the path of "getting in touch" with one's intuitive self.[13] It is not surprising then that this can be a somewhat moving personal experience for members of the thinking subgroup in particular, and each person comes through this stage of the workshop at different rates of speed and awareness—and a few not at all. It is therefore important to try to be sensitive to the different needs of the individual participants in the group and help guide them along as they "experience" this portion of the workshop.

It is important to note, however, that a significant percentage of the thinking subgroup members are "transformed" by the experience of getting in touch with their intuitive ability to the point that they are willing to make commitments on follow-up steps they will take to work on developing their intuitive ability further. For example, 35 percent of the thinking subgroup indicated on the evaluation form at the end of the workshop that they would either "work on applying what they had learned on-the-job" or "they would discuss the workshop contents at work" later.[14]

THE CITY OF PHOENIX CASE

Another good case study illustration of how intuitive brain skills can be structured into the decision making process to increase overall productivity is the City of Phoenix. In 1984 I was asked to conduct a workshop on intuitive decision making for several managers of the city.[15] Executives were first tested and identified by brain styles as in the Tenneco case. Managers were then asked to name a real problem they would like to work on that day that had been plaguing the city. One of the issues selected was "how to facilitate accurate reporting of police activities in the media."

The key here was to structure the participants in such a way as to take maximum advantage of the intuitive skills that existed within the group. Here is how this was done. Managers who scored high on intuitive ability were first put together, cross-cutting normal department lines in the city. This group was then asked to develop a list of possible new solutions to the problem at hand. This approach has several advantages. Intuitive managers tend to be more creative. They tend to be more insightful and are able to identify new ways of doing things. They also tend to prefer a collegial, informal style of decision making that functions most easily across normal lines of responsibility. Also, seeking input from other managers inside the city—but outside the police department (or any other department)—often facilitates the generation of new solutions to what had appeared before to be unsolvable problems.

Following the first step, the list of potential solutions that the intuitive management group prepared was subsequently presented to a *separate* group of "thinking" type managers. This approach also has several advantages. As we have seen in Chapter 5, thinking type managers tend to be more analytical and critical. They also tend to be more skilled at assessing the practicality and relevant facts of another manager's proposal more effectively as contrasted with being able to generate new ideas on their own. They also seem to throw cold water on new and creative ideas—often too quickly—which can inhibit the ability of intuitive type managers to function in tandem with them.

The final step was to integrate the two groups of managers at a third meeting chaired by a person who could facilitate the communication between the two different style groups. The purpose here is to help the total group recognize the value of both the intuitive and thinking type input that has thus far been received, and then to go on and fashion out of the total list of suggestions made by each group a practical plan of action that can be implemented. In this particular case,

Exhibit 6.4
How to Integrate Intuitive Brain Skills into the Decision Making Process

Steps to Take	Purpose
Test managers	Identify managers by brain skill so they can be grouped to work most productively.
Structure decision making process	Ensure that brain skills which are identified will be used most productively.
Evaluation	Further improve future rounds of decision making.

I performed this role, but it can easily be performed by another person such as a trained member of the personnel department staff.[16]

Exhibit 6.4 summarizes the decision making process I just described. Organizing the Phoenix city executives so that they dealt with the problem selected guided first and foremost by brain skills—starting with the intuitive group first and across departmental lines without regard for formal job title or responsibility or years of experience working with the city—resulted in a significant number of workable solutions that the police department itself had not thought of! Written evaluations by the participants following the process indicated that "even some of the crusty old administrators thought the technique was excellent."[17]

Although time in this session did not allow use of this technique to work on all the problems which Phoenix city administrators wanted to tackle, the list they themselves generated is itself worthy of note. Exhibit 6.5 summarizes a sample of these issues or problems. Potential for significant increases in productivity exists when an organization can clearly identify and agree on the problems it needs to solve. The potential is still greater when an open communication structure is created that is conducive to their resolution. Structuring brain skills in the manner I just described enabled these city administrators to agree on a list of problems they need to solve. Attacking this list by employing the techniques just described is also likely to produce a practical plan of action for their resolution.

One of the most useful steps in this workshop for individual participants was to take time to evaluate in some detail the actual decision making process they had just gone through right after it was completed. This gives each participant and group type an opportunity to assess the exercise they have just gone through, to reflect on the strengths and weaknesses of their own particular brain style, and to assess how they might benefit from the input of their opposite brain type.

Exhibit 6.5
Sample Issues/Problems Phoenix City Administrators Proposed for Processing

```
* How can we coordinate two departments that have a
  common responsibility?

* How can we develop a system to ensure that information
  distributed to subordinates is being read and
  assimilated?

* Does personnel recruiting and promotion from within
  lead to stagnation?

* Can the city's financial management system (FMS) be
  adapted to meet the budgetary and financial reporting
  needs of the Human Resources Department?

* How can preconditioned negative response to employee
  organizations be reduced?

* How can top management and mayor/council interest be
  increased regarding the problem of fair housing?
```

If you were conducting such a workshop in your own organization, you could facilitate this process by having each brain style group record their work on a flip chart or overlay. Have someone observing the style and content of the dialogue of each individual participant and brain style group as it takes place for playback afterward. If available, take a video tape of the proceedings as well.

In this particular case, I had each brain style group record their own recommended solutions to the problem of "how to facilitate accurate reporting of police activities in the media" on a flip chart. I also walked from group to group throughout this exercise recording samples of the dialogue that took place, who made which suggestions and when, and how the group processed this input—all for playback and evaluation as soon as the exercise was completed. Then, I asked each participant to observe how the flip charts each group produced appeared to be directly correlated with their "going in" brain style. For example, the list of suggestions coming from the intuitive group tended to be longer and did not match the list of the thinking group. I then asked the workshop members to examine how the total group product was improved still further when the intuitive and thinking group flip chart lists were integrated together at the third stage in the process. Finally, we explored how personal brain styles served either to facilitate or to hinder the overall group product (e.g., judging negatively a new idea too quickly before the group as a whole had a real chance to discuss it; degree of receptivity to a new idea being determined more by the sex of the person offering it than the quality of the idea itself).

CONCLUDING COMMENTS AND OBSERVATIONS

These two case studies would appear to indicate that intuitive decision making can be taught effectively in applied workshop settings such as these. The techniques mentioned here and in the preceding chapters are particularly effective in this process. However, this is not to suggest that every participant is receptive to either the subject of intuition or the techniques outlined here for its further use and development. In fact, experience gained from conducting these and other similar workshops for a wide variety of other organizations across the country has taught me that great care needs to be exercised in teaching this subject including decisions as to which techniques to employ.

BSM assessments themselves can be used as a helpful guide in this process. For example, if the group as a whole that you wish to work with leans predominantly toward thinking scores, you can expect highly critical questions about the subject of intuition itself and also concerning a number of the techniques outlined here. Several of these same participants may be extremely reluctant at the outset to even engage in exercises such as meditation or self-hypnosis. On the other hand, high intuition scoring participants will be more than likely pressing you to move along faster and more deeply into this subject matter.

Before designing the particular training program that should be used in your organization, it is recommended that you decide first what your goals are for intuition training, and how you hope to accomplish them. It would also be helpful to determine the extent of freedom and support you presently have in your organization for starting such a program. Assuming for the moment that your overall goal is to achieve increased productivity in your organization at both an individual and group level, there are several ways you can accomplish this objective. Therefore, it would be a good operating rule of thumb that the greater the resistance you expect or anticipate getting from starting an intuition training program, the slower and more selective you should be about how and where to start the program within your organization. For example, you might wish to begin informally at first with colleagues that you know and trust, and then branch out later to include other high intuitive scoring executives who are most likely to be receptive to such an overture. I would recommend leaving the high thinking scoring executives to the end under these circumstances.

The same can be said for the specific techniques you decide to employ in the training process. Another good operating rule of thumb would be that the more the total group you are seeking to work with leans toward predominantly thinking scores, the more your initial training should include supportive documentation describing the research base upon which your program is founded. For example, it might be helpful to prepare a hand-out outlining who is conducting the leading research on this subject, where it is being conducted, and what the major findings are for distribution at the outset of your training sessions. It probably would also be helpful to start first with developmental exercises that are least "personally threatening" to these participants, and move gradually along as you sense their willingness to take more significant steps. On the other hand, if the group you are working with leans toward intuitive scores, you should be able to pick up the pace considerably. You will need to spend less time explaining why you are using a particular technique or answering questions as to the statistical evidence that proves that it works. High intuitive scorers tend to understand instinctively that what you are doing does or does not make sense. If what you propose to them works, they will use it—simple as that!

Most management groups at the moment tend to lean toward higher thinking scores than intuitive scores on average. However, as we have seen, this will vary by management level, sex, ethnic background, and occupational specialty. As a general rule, I find it is most productive starting off "on the left" with test instruments, study findings, and other related facts and information. This approach tends to give thinking managers the symbols they need to hold on to at first before you go over "to the right," if you will, to teach intuitive techniques. You also have several other things going for you in starting out this way. You can give all participants immediate feedback on themselves. This stimulates their interest because no one likes to talk about any subject more than himself/herself. Another advantage is that BSM data give you a quick snapshot of each individual and the group as a whole as well. This is helpful information for you to have in guiding the tone and direction of the balance of your training effort.

If you find from BSM assessments that you have two quite different subgroups to work with (i.e., high intuitive and high thinking groups), it might prove helpful at first to separate these groups and use a different training program for each appropriate to the circumstances and setting at hand. Later, you can take steps to start integrating the two subgroups together for applied problem solving once each respective group has gained confidence in your ability and the overall program you are seeking to implement.

It is quite possible that you will find a few executives in your organization who will be openly hostile to whatever technique or approach you seek to employ. This is most likely to come from high thinking scoring executives. If possible, I would recommend excluding them from your initial training program since they will not be very receptive at this point, and can even serve to disrupt the entire program if they are regular participants. Perhaps later, after you have chalked up a series of documented successes through your program, you might wish to approach these executives once again. Or, it is quite possible they will even approach you once they hear of your success record.

In the final analysis, there is nothing like successful "reality testing" to promote your program. That is, what works works! Therefore, be sure to start at the outset of your effort gathering as much hard evidence as you can concerning your successes, including case studies of actual decisions at work, personal testimonials from your colleagues, and other related information. You might even consider publishing a small newsletter, which can be useful for this purpose.

The appendix of this book contains an outline of materials that you might find helpful in starting your intuition training program. Included there is a sample outline of one training program model that could be used in whole or in part as appropriate for your own organization. Also you will find forms to be used to start an "intuition club" inside and/or outside your organization on either a formal or an informal basis. Finally, the back of this book also contains an annotated bibliography of source materials including books, articles, audio-visual items, and other related information which can serve as one guide for creating the training program appropriate to your individual and organizational needs.

Turn now to the final chapter of this book where I will outline some of my final thoughts on the intuitive decision making process and present an agenda for further research that appears to be required on this subject.

NOTES

1. These represent a wide range of private and public sector organizations. They all are experiencing megatrend type changes in the environment in which they operate. Examples are several companies within the telephone industry (e.g., Mountain Bell Telephone and New Jersey Bell Telephone), Walt Disney Enterprises, and the National Security Agency. On occasion, several different organizations combine resources to bring in speakers on a topic of interest to them which may help them increase their productivity. Examples from each sector are the Institute for Management Studies, which operates out of San Francisco; the Federal Executive Institute, which is located in Charlottesville, Virginia; and the Senior Public Executive Program operated by the Urban Studies Program at Arizona State University in Tempe.

2. *Tenneco: 1983 Annual Report* (Houston, TX: Tenneco, 1984).

3. Ibid., pp. 2–5.

4. "The Tenneco Staff Professional Program" (Houston, TX: Tenneco, 1985).

5. For details on how to conduct a similar workshop including the use of the *AIM Survey* discussed in Chapters 4 and 5, see Weston H. Agor, *AIM Survey: Trainer's Guide* (Bryn Mawr, PA: Organization Design and Development, 1985), which comes with the *Survey*.

6. The fact that total group and by-sex scores are below the national mean for intuition could be a warning sign. Care should be taken to review the recruitment process now operating at Tenneco to determine whether or not it is functioning in such a way that new professionals are being selected who are in fact "like" those already on staff—but who may not be as productive to have for Tenneco's new emerging future.

7. It is not uncommon for this type person to also experience considerable tension before making a decision. Some top executives have called this "analysis paralysis," and charge that business schools are tending to turn out this type of executive at present. See, e.g., the letter to the editor of the *Harvard Business Review* from Victor A. Casebolt, vice president and group executive with the International Paper Company, on page 184 of the January–February 1985 issue.

8. For example, in this workshop, one Tenneco professional came up during the break to discuss his 6–6 tie score. I asked him if he felt my description of what he experienced before making a decision was accurate. His response was yes, and I had the distinct impression it was a great relief to him that he not only could tell me that, but that I understood how he felt. I cannot help but believe that this person was sufficiently

touched by this experience that he will subsequently seek the counseling he may need to increase not only his productivity but also his job satisfaction.

9. As it relates to women in particular, I have advocated that highly intuitive women should start actively selling their brain skills in job interviews or within their present organization just as more traditional skills are at present. Another impact of the megatrends upon us is that it might give an added impetus to the advancement of women to key management positions.

10. For a discussion of these and other related matters, see Ellen Armstrong, "Putting Intuition to Work: How to Succeed in Business by Trusting Your Hunches," *New Age Journal* (December 1985), pp. 32–37 and 81.

11. See "Tenneco Ventures: Handout Exercise" (Houston, TX: Tenneco, Unpublished Workshop Exercise, October 1985).

12. For a discussion of techniques for preventing "group think" from taking place, or to correct the problem if it already exists, see Mark S. Plovnick, Ronald E. Fry, and W. Warner Burke, *Organization Development: Exercises, Cases, and Readings* (Boston: Little, Brown, 1982), and Stephen K. Blumberg, *Win–Win Administration: How to Manage an Organization So Everybody Wins* (Sun Lakes, AZ: Thomas Horton & Daughters, 1983).

13. For a discussion of this process, see Frances E. Vaughan, *Awakening Intuition* (Garden City, NY: Anchor Books, 1979).

14. These were two of the standard questions used by Tenneco, Inc., in their evaluation process at the end of each workshop. See "Evaluation Forms A & B: Staff Professional Program" (Houston, TX: Tenneco, 1985).

15. This workshop for the City of Phoenix was organized by the Advanced Public Executive Program at Arizona State University in January 1984.

16. Assuming the person selected to perform this role has the training required, it probably would also be helpful to use BSM scores to select the person. For example, a person who has the personality and style to empathize with and value input received from both factual and feeling cues would probably be particularly effective in this role.

17. Letter to the author from the then director of the Advanced Public Executive Program dated January 1984 and also personal letters received from participants after the workshop was completed.

PART III. Agenda for Future Research

CHAPTER 7. The Logic of Intuitive Decision Making: An Agenda for Future Research

The role and importance of intuition in decision making have been acknowledged throughout the ages of man.[1] In more modern times, many practicing executives and scholars alike have posited that intuition is not only a brain skill that is partially inherited, but also one that can be trained and expanded for applied use in management.[2] Despite this fact, it is startling to find that there is little in the way of applied research on this subject. Putting aside many of the more popularized treatments of intuition in the literature today,[3] there are only a small handful of serious scholarly works on the subject. Of these, the majority are essentially theoretical in nature and tend to be produced almost exclusively by psychologists or psychophysiologists.[4] Interdisciplinary research on intuition is virtually non-existent, and field research in actual applied management settings is equally sparse.

For the studies which do exist, the very design and focus of them are equally disconcerting. As a rule, for example, the researchers who carry out this work often give their studies such titles as "paranormal" or "non-rational processes."[5] What this really means is that the "hard scientists" who have taken up this subject for research cannot yet explain or measure successfully the precise process by which intuition works—even though there is at the same time a ready amount of hard evidence to indicate the process itself does exist.[6] Rather than admit this fact—and thereby the very limits of hard science technology itself at this point in its development—non-neutral labels are assigned to work on this subject instead. This tends to discourage serious research on intuition and/or acceptability in the scientific community even when significant findings are actually presented.[7]

The very design of several of these research studies also makes it difficult to obtain regularly reliable results that are acceptable to the broader scientific community and/or that satisfy the demands from potential financial supporters for evidence of the practical usefulness of this work. For example, a large body of research has involved asking subjects to demonstrate greater than chance ability to read card numbers and colors that another subject is looking at—or other similar repetitive tasks.[8] Much of this work has been conducted under highly controlled laboratory conditions. The problem with this design is that the experimental subject quickly loses interest in such repetitive and routine tasks, and his/her record of success correspondingly declines. Potential government and private sector research sponsors ask how this rather antiseptically designed work can be used in some practical way to justify its support to watchful congressmen or stockholders.[9]

At the very same time, we are on the threshold of achieving major advances in our understanding of how the human brain functions. Already, replication of some of the more elementary and routine functions of the brain has spawned a whole new field known as ''artificial intelligence,'' which is working with some success to develop ways of putting research findings to practical and applied use.[10] These and other new breakthroughs which can be expected in the next decade all suggest that an investment in developing practical ways for using and increasing our human brain skills to the fullest for applied decision making is likely to pay high dividends.

This is so in large part because we know so little at the moment about how our brain in fact functions and how particular processes like intuition take place and can be encouraged to take place. Unfolding technological advances applied to such a virgin field all suggest enormous upside potential. As one public executive put it recently, the mind and the creative potential of employees represent one of the few remaining resources that can still be expanded. Not using these resources is the same as turning your back on a new revenue source.[11]

AN AGENDA FOR FUTURE RESEARCH

The research I have presented in this book concerning the use of intuition in executive decision making should be regarded as exploratory. An exploratory study is one in which little or no previous research exists. Often, the findings are tentative and could well be later modified through subsequent research. In fact, one of the objectives of this book is to encourage both academic scholars and practicing executives alike to devote more time and resources to the systematic study of intuitive decision making—preferably in more applied and interdisciplinary settings than has been true in the past.

For those who are interested in making such a commitment, I have several thoughts and suggestions for you to consider before proceeding. First, I suggest that you adopt this ''going in mind set'' about the subject of intuition. Take as your working hypothesis that intuition is simply a rational and logical brain skill that can be used to help guide decision making. It is not paranormal. Allow your mind to imagine the possibility that hard science has not yet developed the ability to quantify step-by-step how this process in fact works, but that this capability will be developed sometime during the balance of this century. In the meantime, assume that the process by which intuition works is a highly complex one. Assume that this process involves a series of input sources. Assume that one of these is a series of programs that are hidden in the brain and passed on from generation to generation, something analogous to the migration programs for birds and the survival instincts of other animals.[12]

Assume that other input sources can include either factual and/or feeling cues experienced during this particular lifetime that can also potentially serve as one possible basis for future generational brain programming. Assume that the degree to which input from any or all these potential sources is actually experienced will depend in part on how we process our life(s) through the filters of our own personal and cultural/societal egos.[13] Hence, for example, our definition of "reality" may well depend not only on reality itself as it truly exists, but at least in part on our own perception of reality and/or our willingness to accept what is in fact so—either about ourselves or about the organization in which we work. The more receptive and open we are to the potential cues that exist on all these levels (i.e., factual, feeling, preprogrammed), the greater our "consciousness" is of reality. The greater this consciousness is, the greater is our potential intuitive ability. Whether we "actualize" this potential ability on any or all of the levels discussed in Chapter 1 will also depend on whether we learn to "actualize" or bring it "on line" on command. This takes practice. Some of the ways to achieve this facility appear to be through the techniques outlined in this book—on both an individual and a group level. Other avenues are yet to be discovered.

Quantitative hard science research concerning how the intuitive process in fact works step-by-step will take a major effort spanning several years. For research of such magnitude to be both meaningful and supported by potential funding sources, it will have to demonstrate practical and applied results in both the short and the long term. In order to accomplish this goal, several suggestions seem plausible. First, the effort should be global and interdisciplinary in scope. The very best minds in all the various disciplines will be required to unravel one of the brain's greatest puzzles, and the nature of intuition itself also demands an interdisciplinary understanding. Second, the establishment of a global "intuition network" to facilitate this process would also seem to be a highly productive step to take (see the appendix for more details). This network would have several advantages. The latest findings could be instantaneously transmitted worldwide by such means as computer or satellite hookups. Unnecessary duplication and overlap of studies could be avoided while helping to ensure that research is also designed to build upon earlier work already successfully completed. Some of the destructive potential applications of intuitive brain skills could, it is hoped, be minimized through such an open sharing process as well.[14]

Finally, efforts should be made to enlist the participation and support of successful highly intuitive executives around the world for the establishment of this intuition network. No single step will generate more support—whether financial or otherwise. For example, if some of these executives could be encouraged to speak out openly about their intuitive ability and how they use their ability to make decisions, others would be encouraged to do likewise. A major global resource would thereby be developed for more systematic study and development. If these executives would also be willing to be studied more carefully by interdisciplinary teams of researchers, we could well learn more effectively about how the intuitive process in fact works by level of application. Similarly, if organizations themselves through their own efforts would adopt internal programs designed to assess and evaluate the intuitive processes of their management staff and report to the network regularly on their successes and failures, general financial support for ongoing research from traditional funding sources would probably be soon forthcoming.

It is also recommended that before scholars or laboratory scientists begin to carry out their proposed study designs on this subject, they solicit the review and comment of a panel of these highly intuitive executives who are willing to participate in this manner. This process could well focus research efforts more effectively to help ensure immediate short-term payouts in the form of findings that can be practically used by their organizations themselves which in turn will help to generate further financial support for more extensive long-term projects. Another outcome of this review process could be that totally new directions in research will be suggested that are highly plausible but never thought of by the scientists concerned (or pursued even when so)—quite possibly because they tend to be predominantly thinking types themselves.

Some thought should also be given to whether research on intuitive processes should not also include in the study design young children and students in private and public sector management programs at the university level besides practicing intuitive executives. There has been a growing body of research to suggest, for example, that young children are far more intuitive than adults, but soon learn to suppress and/or "unlearn" this ability as a result of our current models of classroom instruction as well as through societal pressures.[15] Longitudinal study designs encompassing these different age groups might unlock other clues to our understanding of how the intuitive process works and can be developed further. Similarly, the study of gifted children in this regard might provide still other clues. For example, some of the recent research by Howard Gardner and D. N. Perkins suggests that our traditional notions about human intelligence and how it is acquired are only "partial glimpses" of reality at best.[16] One might well speculate whether precocious children's early ability is really one manifestation of the fact that man does have some form of programmed knowledge at birth that complements knowledge acquired by more traditional means during this lifetime. Or, do the newer theories of quantum physics suggest still other explanations for ways we can learn "to tap into" our intuitive pool of knowledge more systematically?[17]

Other pieces to understanding the intuitive puzzle may well be found through the study of how our brain stores and forgets information accumulated—including genetically from generation to generation. The latest research available on this process, for example, suggests that some of the previous scientific notions about it held by such famous psychologists as Sigmund Freud are at least partially incorrect [18] When it comes right down to it, at this very moment we know that the brain has the capacity to create totally new synaptic connections as a result of electrical impulses generated through outside stimuli from life experiences. These synaptic connections become our new knowledge, awareness, or extended capabilities beyond those that we started with when this process began.[19] How this all works precisely step-by-step—or can be facilitated—is still largely an unfolding mystery.[20]

In closing, I cannot help but wonder whether our research on these and other related questions will not only enable us to better understand how the intuitive process itself works, but also thereby help lead us to discover new and better ways of enhancing the well being of all mankind on this planet. Perhaps greater productivity and happiness will be achievable worldwide when we all learn how to integrate the intuitive processes of the Eastern world with the deductive analytical processes emphasized in the Western world within ourselves, our organizations, and our universe.

NOTES

1. *Metaphysical Bible Dictionary* (Unity Village, MO: Unity School of Christianity, 1931).

2. For a recent treatment of several leading researchers in this field working on applied uses of intuition in management, see Ellen Armstrong, "Putting Intuition to Work: How to Succeed in Business by Trusting Your Hunches," *New Age Journal* (December 1985), pp. 32–37 and 81. Also see John Naisbitt's treatment of this subject in John Naisbitt and Patricia Aburdene, *Reinventing the Corporation* (New York: Warner Books, 1985).

3. Some examples are Milton Fisher, *Intuition: How to Use It for Success and Happiness* (New York: E. P. Dutton, 1981), and Flora Davis, *Inside Intuition: What We Know About Nonverbal Communication* (New York: Signet Books, 1973).

4. See, e.g., Malcolm Westcott, *Toward a Contemporary Psychology of Intuition: A Historical, Theoretical, and Empirical Approach* (New York: Holt, Rinehart & Winston, 1968); Frances Vaughan, *Awakening Intuition* (Garden City, NY: Anchor Books, 1979); and Tony Bastick, *Intuition: How We Think and Act* (New York: John Wiley & Sons, 1982).

5. A recent title of a serious research study in a series of many at Princeton University's School of Engineering was entitled "On the Quantum Mechanics of Consciousness, with Applications to Anomalies Phenomena" (Princeton, NJ: Princeton University, June 1984 revision). The very title of the laboratory where this research is being conducted is the Princeton Engineering Anomalies Research Laboratory. Another book of articles is Owen Davies, ed., *The Omni Book of the Paranormal and the Mind* (New York: Kensington Publishing Co., 1982). These titles for laboratories and research are what I mean.

6. Duke University conducted research for years. More recently Russell Targ, Harold Puthoff, and Keith Harary in northern California and Stephen Schwartz and Rand De Mattei in southern California have been active. A recently published paper in a respected hard science outlet on this subject was Robert G. Jahn, "The Persistent Paradox of Psychic Phenomena: An Engineering Perspective," *Proceedings of the IEEE* 70, 2 (February 1982) pp. 136–70. For another summary in policy circles, see Christopher H.

Dodge, "Research into 'Psi' Phenomena: Current Status and Trends of Congressional Concern" (Washington, DC: Congressional Research Service, Library of Congress, June 2, 1983).

7. See, e.g., Russell Targ and Keith Harary, *The Mind Race: Understanding and Using Psychic Abilities* (New York: Villard Books, 1984).

8. Much of the research conducted by J. B. Rhine at Duke University was of this type for years.

9. Some of the U.S. government support of Stanford Research Institute research fell into hard times for this very reason.

10. For a recent discussion of this topic and also the role of intuition in the process, see the interview with John Seely Brown in Loren MacArthur, "Artificial Intelligence," *Southwest Airlines Magazine* (October 1985), pp. 84–89 and 120.

11. Ed Everett, "Improving Creativity—One Organization's Approach," *Public Management* 65, 2 (February 1983), p. 8. A recent article in the *Chronicle of Higher Education* pointed out some of the hot areas for research discoveries today are decision theory and work having to do with the brain, according to the current president of the American Psychological Association. See "Major Trends in Research: 22 Leading Scholars Report on Their Fields," *Chronicle of Higher Education* (September 4, 1985), pp. 12–13.

12. Laurence R. Sprecher, a consultant with Public Management Associates in Oregon, has suggested this view of intuition in a letter to the editor in *Public Management* 65, 2 (February 1983), p. 18.

13. For an extensive treatment of this particular orientational model of the subject of intuition, see several selections in Roger N. Walsh and Frances Vaughan, eds., *Beyond Ego: Transpersonal Dimensions in Psychology* (Los Angeles: J. P. Tarcher, 1980).

14. For a discussion of some of the potentially destructive aspects, see Targ and Harary, *The Mind Race*, pp. 247–60.

15. See Alex Tanous and Katherine Fair Donnelly, *Is Your Child Psychic? A Guide for Creative Parents and Teachers* (New York: Macmillan, 1979).

16. See Howard Gardner, *Frames of Mind: The Theory of Multiple Intelligences* (New York: Basic Books, 1983), and D. N. Perkins, *The Mind's Best Work* (Cambridge, MA: Harvard University Press, 1981).

17. Fritjof Capra, *The Tao of Physics*, 2nd ed. (Boulder, CO: Shambhala, 1983); Fred Alan Wolf, *Star Wave: Mind, Consciousness and Quantum Physics* (New York: Macmillan, 1984).

18. See the public television program "Learning and Memory" in the series on the brain produced with the support of the Annenberg Foundation in 1984; this is also available for lease or purchase nationwide. In this program, research is presented that questions Freud's notion that childhood memories cannot be recalled because they are simply painful. Another probability is that one *normal* process of the brain is "to forget" unimportant information in order to allow space for new more important information necessary for survival. How this same process might relate to remembering or forgetting earlier life experiences and regression therapy is intriguing, and could well provide some of the explanations we are looking for to how intuition works.

19. Ibid.

20. Equally relevant to our understanding could well be learning how it is that human beings (and animals) learn "to calibrate" to each other over time, and why sibling pairs seem to have greater ability to communicate with each other than the average brother or sister.

Appendix

This appendix contains three items:

- an outline of a "model intuition program" that you can consider implementing in your own organization as described in Chapters 5 and 6;
- intuition network forms that you can use to establish an "intuition club" in your organization as described in Chapter 5, and/or to join a global intuition network as discussed in Chapter 7;
- an open-ended questionnaire used to survey highly intuitive top executives during 1984–85 as described in Chapter 3.

Outline of a Model Intuition Program

STEPS TO TAKE   RESOURCES RECOMMENDED

I. Cognitive Awareness Testing

    A. Implement a BSM Testing   AIM Survey and MBTI

        Program Appropriate to   discussed in Chapters

        Your Objective.   4 and 5.

    B. Practice Self Awareness   Self Awareness

        Exercises.   Exercises in Chapter 4.

    C. Explore Other Techniques   Cassette tapes and

        • Journal Keeping   books by Frances

        • Exchange in "Intuition   Vaughan and Jean Bolen

          Club"   in the annotated

        • Read about experiences   bibliography in this

          of others   book, and the

                                  resources cited at

                                  the end of the AIM

                                  Survey.

II. Integrate Intuitive Ability Into

    Daily Decision Making

    A. Program For Use of   Chapters 5 and 6 of

        Intuition at Work.   this book; Chapter 3

        1. Locate and Use   of my book, Intuitive

            Intuitive Talent on   Management; and my

Problems Where Brain   video and cassette

Skill Is Best Suited.   tapes in the annotated

                              bibliography.

2. Integrate Intuitive

    Input with More

    Traditional Management

    Techniques.

B. Establish a Data Base   Chapter 7.

    Program to Assess the

    Productivity of Intuitive

    Input and Decision Making.

III. Systematically Develop Intuitive

      Talent for Applied Use

      A. Establish "Intuition Club"   Appendix forms.

          at Work.

      B. Join Worldwide Intuition   Appendix forms.

          Network.

      C. Adopt New Organizational   Chapter 5.

          Model and Management

          Practices for Decision

          Making.

      D. Provide Financial Support   Chapter 7.

          for Research on Intuition.

Model Intuition Club Registration Form

We are establishing an "intuition club" at

_____ in order to help locate, use,
(name of your organization)
and develop this brain skill talent for applied use. It is

our belief that intuition is one management skill which will

be increasingly important to our organization and its

capacity to meet the "megatrend" challenges already facing

us now and in the future.

I solicit your talent and your personal participation.

Please complete the form provided below at your earliest

convenience and return it to _____.
                            (designated official)

                            Sincerely,

                            Organizational Officer

Name   _____

Address or   _____

Stop   _____

Phone Number   (   ) _____

Please indicate why you are personally interested in joining

this club.

_____

_____

_____

_____

Please indicate any special intuitive skill or ability you believe you possess that would be helpful to our organization. If you have specific examples that you can give from past experience in this regard, please do so.

_____

_____

_____

_____

_____

Global Intuition Network

Individual or Organization Registration Form

The purpose of the "Global Intuition Network" is simple: promote the applied use of intuition in decision making; share new knowledge on how to use this brain skill as it becomes known; and promote ongoing research on intuitive processes for practical use in organizations. Once fully established, it is anticipated that a computer exchange network will be used to facilitate this process, and regular conventions will also be held for this purpose.

Please type or print the information requested below. Mail this form to: Weston H. Agor, President, ENFP Enterprises, 6022 Caprock, #103, El Paso, Texas 79912. If you have any questions, you may also call 915-581-2532.

Name _____

Address _____

_____

_____

Phone Number _____ (   ) _____

Preference (indicate one)

Join Network in my area _____

Organize Network in my area _____

Register My Organization Network _____

For Organizations Already Established Only

A. Primary Program Objectives and Activities Established

_____

_____

_____

_____

B. Please indicate the names, addresses, and phone numbers
    of your network group members below. List first the
    person who is primarily responsible for organizing the
    group.

Name   Address   Phone Number
_____   _____   _____

_____   _____   _____

_____   _____   _____

_____   _____   _____

_____   _____   _____

_____   _____   _____

_____   _____   _____

_____   _____   _____

The Intuitive Manager Survey Questionnaire

Over 3,000 executives have been tested nationally for their intuitive ability using selected questions from the intuition-sensing portion of the Myers-Briggs Type Indicator (described in Chapter 2). For those executives who scored in the top 10 percent on the intuition scale constructed from these questions, a second open-ended survey questionnaire was prepared in order to determine whether/how they used their intuitive ability to guide important organizational decisions (discussed in Chapter 3). The original questionnaire for the second part of this study is presented here for your review.

Based on the findings from this research, a totally revised survey instrument has now been prepared entitled, Test Your Intuitive Powers: AIM Survey (Bryn Mawr, PA: Organization Design and Development, 1985). See Chapter 4 for details on this instrument and how to use it in BSM programs.

Original Open-Ended Questionnaire

This short test is designed to help you as a highly intuitive manager determine for yourself how you go about making decisions on-the-job and/or in your personal life.

The test is also designed to help you get "in touch with" any particular techniques/methods (if any) that you may be using on a regular basis to help you to develop your intuitive ability further.

1. Do you believe you use intuition to guide your most important decisions?

   Yes_____   No_____

2. If yes, how do you go about using your intuition to make your most important decisions? Please be specific.

   _____

   _____

   _____

   _____

   _____

   _____

3. How does your intuition tell you that a particular decision is "right" or "wrong"? (e.g., what kind of feelings/signals do you get or regularly rely on for cues)

   _____

   _____

   _____

   _____

   _____

4. Can you give me an example or two of a very important
    decision where you followed your intuition and it
    proved to be the <u>right</u> one?

    _____

    _____

    _____

    _____

    _____

    _____

5. Can you give me an example or two of a very important
    decision where you followed your intuition and it
    proved to be the <u>wrong</u> one?

    _____

    _____

    _____

    _____

    _____

6. Thinking back now about these times, can you pinpoint
    any specific factors about yourself or your surroundings
    which seemed to exist or be present when your decision
    appeared to:

    <u>Be Right</u>

    _____

    _____

<u>Be Wrong</u>

_____

_____

_____

7. Do you tend to "keep it a secret" that you use intuition
    to make decisions, or do you feel comfortable sharing
    this fact with others?

    Keep It A Secret _____   Share With Others _____

    <u>Please Explain</u>

    _____

    _____

    _____

    _____

    _____

8. When using your intuition, have you found that it
    functions best only with <u>certain</u> problems/issues/
    circumstances or do you use it freely to help guide <u>all</u>
    your major decisions?

    Certain Matters Only _____   All Decisions _____

    <u>Please Explain</u>

    _____

    _____

    _____

9. When making a major decision, do you use any particular
    technique or method(s) to help draw on your intuitive
    ability more effectively?

        Yes_____   No_____

    If Yes, Please Describe

    _____

    _____

    _____

    _____

    _____

    _____

10. Do you use or practice regularly any particular
    technique or method(s) to help develop your intuitive
    ability further?

        Yes_____   No_____

    If Yes, Please Describe

    _____

    _____

    _____

    _____

    _____

    _____

11. If you have any additional information or thoughts that
     now come to mind that <u>you</u> <u>feel</u> are important, record
     them for yourself here now.

     _____

     _____

     _____

     _____

     _____

     _____

Glossary of Selected Terms

Intuition—You will find many definitions for intuition in the literature. The one presented here is the same as that used by Frances E. Vaughan, psychologist and author of the book, *Awakening Intuition*, which is cited in the bibliography.

A way of knowing, recognizing the possibilities in any situation. Extrasensory perception, clairvoyance, telepathy, psychometry, remote viewing, and psychokinesis are all manifestations of intuitive ability on one level or another. There are four levels of intuitive awareness: physical, emotional, mental, and spiritual.

For details, see Chapter 1.

Parapsychology—The branch of science that deals with psi communication.

PK (Psychokinesis)—The extramotor aspect of psi; a direct (i.e., mental) influence exerted by the subject on an external physical object, process, or condition.

Precognition—Prediction of future events, i.e., random events, the occurrence of which cannot be inferred from present knowledge.

Psi (Parapsychical, Parapsychological)—Extrasensorimotor exchange with the environment. Psi based on the definition above would be the same thing as intuition fully developed on all levels.

Psi phenomena—Occurrences that result from the operation of psi or intuition.

Psychometry—Ability to obtain information by touching or handling a person or object.

Quantum physics—The basis by which intuition takes place. An understanding of quantum physics will provide an understanding of intuition.

Remote viewing—Ability to describe a faraway place or object never actually seen or experienced oneself; primarily an ability to process pictorial, non-analytical information received.

Significance—A numerical result is significant when it equals or surpasses a criterion or degree of chance probability: normally either odds of at least five in one hundred or one in one hundred.

Synchronicity—An acausal connection between two independent events, when two independent events not causally connected combine to have a third meaning.

Telepathy—The mental level of intuition; the ability to communicate mentally with another person. A sender is one who sends information and a receiver is one who accepts this information.

Annotated Bibliography of Resources on Intuition

This annotated bibliography is organized around Part II of this book, "Implementing a Program for Using and Developing Intuition to Increase Organizational Productivity." It is divided into two basic sections to be used along with Chapters 4 and 5 accordingly. I have included materials that will not only help you to assess your intuitive ability, but will also assist you in implementing a BSM program in your organization. Books, articles, test instruments, audio-visual materials, and other related information are included here for your review and assistance. Of course, the ultimate decision as to what you actually use depends on what you feel most comfortable with personally.

I. USING AND DEVELOPING YOUR INTUITIVE BRAIN SKILLS

This section is divided into three parts. The first part deals primarily with "what intuition is," the second part with traditional and non-traditional tests which you may use to measure this skill, and finally examples of actual intuitive executives and how they use their ability for applied decision making, which I think you will find useful to help you "get in touch" with your own ability. For purposes of organizing this section, I am using the definition of intuition in the glossary of terms in this book.

A. What Intuition Is

Books

Agee, Doris. *Edgar Cayce on ESP*. New York: Warner Books, 1969. Describes the various levels of intuition that can be found in the records of Edgar Cayce's work. Cayce, now deceased, was a famous and gifted intuitive who often used his powers to find health cures for clients when traditional medicine appeared to fail.

Bastick, Tony. *Intuition: How We Think and Act*. New York: John Wiley & Sons, 1982. Highly technical but also valuable approach to the subject. This book is an effort to build a scientific theory of intuition that can be used to guide research. Summarizes some of the most recent research on the topic.

Berne, Eric. *Intuition and Ego States*. San Francisco: T. A. Press, 1977. Compilation of papers on the topic by the author of *Games People Play* that later led to his approach to psychotherapy called *transactional analysis*.

Blakeslee, Thomas R. *The Right Brain: A New Understanding of the Unconscious Mind and Its Creative Powers*. New York: Berkeley Books, 1983. Discusses the latest split brain research and the role the right brain plays in our learning. Recommends integrated processes of thinking.

Bolen, Jean Shimoda. *The Tao of Psychology: Synchronicity and the Self*. San Francisco: Harper & Row, 1979. Discusses this Jungian concept with examples from her own private practice. Particularly useful as a guide to the spiritual level of intuition.

Cayce, Hugh Lynn. *Venture Inward: The Incredible Story of Edgar Cayce*. New York: Harper & Row, 1964. Guide to opening intuition beyond consciousness, the ways such insight can be achieved, and the dangers of some.

Davies, Owen, ed. *The Omni Book of the Paranormal and the Mind*. New York: Kensington Publishing Co., 1982. Wide-ranging book of readings including articles on the many levels of intuitive awareness that are possible.

Davis, Flora. *Inside Intuition: What We Know About Nonverbal Communication*. Garden City, NY: Anchor Books, 1979. Essentially treats the ability to read non-verbal cues, which is an intuitive skill.

Dean, Douglas, and John Mihalasky. *Executive ESP*. Englewood Cliffs, NJ: Prentice-Hall, 1974. Discusses test and results of work with CEOs that showed those who had precognitive ability also had the highest profit record.

Fisher, Milton. *Intuition: How to Use It for Success and Happiness*. New York: E. P. Dutton, 1981. Popularized introduction to the subject. Reading list may be of interest.

Fuller, R. Buckminster. *Intuition*. San Luis Obispo, CA: Impact Publishers, 1983. A relatively loose and free swinging treatment of the subject. Probably the most useful section concerns his discussion about the difference between the mind and the brain.

Gibson, Sandra. *Beyond the Body*. New York: Tower, 1979. Story of a young woman who discovered she possessed highly intuitive ability as chronicled from her journal. The technique used to unblock her was hypnotherapy.

Goldberg, Philip. *The Intuitive Edge: Understanding and Developing Intuition*. Los Angeles: J. P. Tarcher, 1983. Treats the broad subject of how an intuitive person thinks. Contains a how-to-develop-the-skill section.

Hayward, Jeremy W. *Perceiving Ordinary Magic: Science and Intuitive Wisdom*. Boulder, CO: New Science Library, 1984. Discusses how our own belief system conditions what we are able and willing to perceive.

Karagulla, Shafica. *Breakthrough to Creativity: Your Higher Sense Perception*. Marina del Rey, CA: De Vorss, 1967. Eight years of research with "sensitives' " ability to use intuition in a variety of ways.

McRae, Ronald W. *Mind Wars: The True Story of Secret Government Research into the Military Potential of Psychic Weapons*. New York: St. Martin's Press, 1984. Discusses military experimentation with particular levels of intuitive ability including psychokinesis and remote viewing.

Ostrander, Sheila, and Lynn Schroeder. *Psychic Discoveries Behind the Iron Curtain*.

New York: Bantam Books, 1970. Reports on the research concerning one intuitive skill—extrasensory perception—behind the iron curtain.

Progoff, Ira. *Jung, Synchronicity, and Human Destiny: Noncausal Dimensions of Human Experience*. New York: Delta, 1973. Discusses the famous psychologist Carl Jung's late-in-life work on synchronicity, that is, "when two or more events, each with its own causality, come together for no apparent reason to produce a third result."

Psychic. Psychics: In-Depth Interviews. New York: Harper & Row, 1972. Interviews by the editors of the now-defunct magazine called *Psychic*, which has since become *New Realities*.

Robbins, Shawn. *Ahead of Myself: Confessions of a Professional Psychic*. Englewood Cliffs, NJ: Prentice-Hall, 1980. Personal experiences of a professional intuitive person, and how she learned to deal with her gifts, with suggestions for you, too.

Salk, Jonas. *Anatomy of Reality: Merging of Intuition and Reason*. New York: Columbia University Press, 1983. The most interesting part of this book is Salk's discussion of how he used his intuition to guide his most important scientific discoveries.

Tanous, Alex, and Katherine Fair Donnelly. *Is Your Child Psychic?: A Guide for Creative Parents and Teachers*. New York: Macmillan, 1979. A very useful book which is recommended not only to understand but to encourage a child's intuitive development. Games and exercises for this purpose are included.

Targ, Russell, and Keith Harary. *The Mind Race: Understanding and Using Psychic Abilities*. Palo Alto, CA: Villard Books, 1984. Reports in large part on the Stanford Research Institute remote viewing experiments but also discusses other applications including intuition in business.

Targ, Russell, and Harold Putoff. *Mind-Reach: Scientists Look at Psychic Ability*. New York: Dell, 1977. Discusses experiments examined by two physicists that involved two intuitive skills—extrasensory perception and remote viewing.

Vaughan, Alan. *The Edge of Tomorrow: How to Foresee and Fulfill Your Future*. New York: Coward, McCann & Geoghegan, 1982. Works on using intuition to foresee the future. Here, he tells you how to develop your talents, too. Vaughan is considered nationally as one of the most accurate predictors by such organizations as Central Premonitions Registry.

Vaughan, Frances E. *Awakening Intuition*. Garden City, NY: Anchor Books, 1979. Written by a transpersonal psychologist. Probably the best book currently available on what intuition is and how to develop it. Her appendix, "Guidelines for Awakening Intuition," is a jewel.

Walsh, Roger N., and Frances E. Vaughan eds. *Beyond Ego: Transpersonal Dimensions in Psychology*. Los Angeles: J. P. Tarcher, 1980. Discusses the emergence of a transpersonal perspective worldwide, and techniques for facilitating this process.

Westcott, Malcolm R. *Toward a Contemporary Psychology of Intuition: A Historical, Theoretical, and Empirical Inquiry*. New York: Holt, Rinehart & Winston, 1968. Discusses various historical definitions for intuition rooted in both philosophy and psychology. Goes on to empirically test a college student population for intuitive problem solving ability. Ends by arguing for the importance of further studies on intuition and the practical relevance of this skill in the age we are entering.

Yeterian, Dixie. *Casebook of a Psychic Detective*. New York: Stein & Day, 1982.

Discusses her life and the law enforcement cases she has used her psychic skills to help solve.

Articles

"Almost Everyone Has Psychic Abilities." *U.S. News and World Report* (May 7, 1984), p. 73. Article about the research work of Keith Harary and Russell Targ on remote viewing.

Assaglioli, Roberto. "Self-Realization and Psychological Disturbances." *Mandalama Journal* (August 1981), pp. 4–11. Discusses the steps to superconsciousness and the experiences that help you to know you are both on your way and also okay.

Browder, Sue. "Women's Intuition: Our Formidable Advantage." *Cosmopolitan* (April 1983), pp. 235–37. Discusses the topic in popularized manner with test included.

Cornell, James. "Science vs. the Paranormal." *Psychology Today* (March 1984), pp. 28–33. Outlines the work of Paul Kurtz to debunk paranormal claims that are not well grounded in scientific procedure. Shows the importance of both keeping an open mind but also of following rigorous thinking type procedures whenever possible.

Coughlin, Ellen K. "Separating the Science of the Paranormal from the Magic and the Metaphysics of It." *Chronicle of Higher Education* (June 19, 1985), pp. 7–9. Discusses the new chair created in parapsychology at the University of Edinburgh. Robert L. Morris, who will take this chair, states that parapsychology should be regarded as an interdisciplinary problem area. One of the reasons research support is hard to come by in this area is the very labels used to describe it, such as "paranormal."

Dodge, Christopher H. "Research into 'Psi' Phenomena: Current Status and Trends of Congressional Concern." Washington, DC: Congressional Research Service, Library of Congress, June 2, 1983. Research paper. Surveys the present research being conducted on psi phenomena in the United States and other countries, and discusses the possible implications for government and society.

Goleman, Daniel. "New View of Unconscious Gives It Expanded Role." *New York Times* (February 7, 1984), pp. C1-C2. Describes how intuitive processes work in part based on recent research.

Guillen, Michael A. "The Intuitive Edge." *Psychology Today* (August 1984), pp. 68–69. Discusses what intuition is and practical applications to learning.

Hathaway, Nancy. "Intuition: How You Can Recognize It and Make It Work for You." *San Francisco Chronicle* (October 31, 1984), p. cc1. One of the interesting studies reported in this article is on Harvard research which shows that when decision makers use intuition, their physical responses vary from those during normal logical decision making processes.

Jahn, Robert G. "The Persistent Paradox of Psychic Phenomena: An Engineering Perspective." *Proceedings of the IEEE* 70, 2 (February 1982), pp. 136–70. Discusses the engineering research on this subject written by the Princeton University Dean of the College of Engineering.

Jahn, Robert G., and Brenda J. Dunne "On the Quantum Mechanics of Consciousness, With Applications to Anomolies Phenomena." Princeton, NJ: Princeton University, June 1984 revision. Seeks to apply the new theories of quantum physics to explain "phychic" phenomena observed in controlled scientific experiments.

Keutzer, Carolin S. "The Power of Meaning: From Quantum Mechanics to Synchronicity." *Journal of Humanistic Psychology* 24, 1 (Winter 1984), pp. 80–94. The startling and paradoxical discoveries in quantum mechanics and the Jungian concepts of acausality and synchronicity are examined in terms of their parallels and their implications for our personal lives.

Murphy, Thomas P. "Eureka!" *Forbes Magazine* (May 7, 1984), p. 218. Describes Dr. Morris I. Stein's research on creativity. This psychologist finds that intuition and creativity are linked.

Prince, George. "Creativity and Learning Skills, Not Talents." *Phillips Exeter Bulletin* (June–July and September–October 1980), reprint. Explains the difference between left brain and right brain thinking styles and skills. Useful as a general background so that you can see where the intuitive function can fit in your overall thinking patterns.

"Psychic Lab Experiments with the Unmeasurable." Gannett News Service (October 23, 1985). Outlines research being conducted at one center in the United States on psychokinesis in San Antonio, Texas.

Robbins, Shawn. "Those Subtle Little Voices Within." *New Woman Magazine* (October 1982), pp. 64–68. Section on how to develop your intuition from her book cited above.

"Scientist Donates $40-Million to U. of Illinois for Research on Intelligence." *Chronicle of Higher Education* (October 9, 1985), p. 29. This is one demonstration of the interdisciplinary research efforts to come that are likely to generate major new information about how the brain functions in this next decade.

Sperry, Roger. "Some Effects of Disconnecting the Cerebral Hemispheres." Nobel Lecture, December 8, 1981. Lecture by the Nobel Prize winner on this split brain research that became popularized as left brain and right brain thinking. Recently this work is being questioned as being oversimplified. It is questionable that all of our intuitive insights simply come from only one area of the brain.

"The Spring Hill Education Conference Issue." *Institute of Noetic Sciences Newsletter* (Spring 1982). Covers treatment of conference on exploration concerning the untapped potential we have in the total field of intuition.

Truzzi, Marcello. "China's Psychic Savants." *Omni* (January 1985), pp. 62ff. Discusses recent controlled research of supposedly gifted psychic children in China which did not meet controlled scientific conditions. Demonstrates the importance of integrating good methodological techniques with intuitive skills for quality performance.

"The Two Sides of the Brain." *Science* (April 1983), pp. 488–90. Summarizes recent research on behavioral asymmetries and their link to physical asymmetries in the brain.

Vaughan, Frances E. "What Is Intuition?" *New Realities* (Spring 1982), pp. 16–22. Essentially a summary of her book above, along with quotes from people who use intuition in various walks of life.

Walker, David. "U. of Edinburgh Wins $1-Million Bequest to Set up Professorship in Parapsychology." *Chronicle of Higher Education* (March 14, 1984), p. 36. An example of some of the new work being supported around the world in this field, and also the difficulties encountered in doing so.

Weintraub, Pamela. "The Brain: His and Hers." *Discover* (April 1981), pp. 15–20. Discusses research suggesting that if men and women do think differently, it may be linked to brain development physically.

Audio-Visual Materials

Adair, Margo. "Intuitive Problem Solving: Cassette Tape Number 1942." San Francisco: New Dimensions Radio, 1985. Discusses what intuitive experiences can be like for some people, and helps also to teach these individuals to feel comfortable with the cues they receive.

Agor, Weston H., and Alan Vaughan. "Using Your Intuition." Hollywood, CA: UMS Television Productions, 1982. Personal interview on the television program "Quest Four" by Damien Simpson. This one hour video tape explains what intuition is, how it can be developed, and discusses some practical applications in organizations. Available from UMS Productions, 3212 E. 8th St., Long Beach, CA 90804.

Bolen, Jean Shimoda. "The Tao of Psychology: Cassette Tape Number 1519." San Francisco: New Dimensions Radio, 1984. Interview with the author of the book by the same name discussing what synchronicity is, with examples from her own private practice.

"Develop Your Psychic Abilities." Alto, MI: Potentials Unlimited, 1978. Cassette tape takes you through steps to practice developing your intuitive skills.

Goldberg, Philip. "Intuition, Imagination and Intelligence, Cassette Tape Number 1847." San Francisco: New Dimensions Radio, 1984. Cassette taped interview with the author of the book *Intuitive Edge* on how he uses this skill in his own writing and how you can use it in yours.

Griswold, Robert E. "Developing Your ESP." Edina, MN: Effective Learning Systems, 1981. Very good cassette tape that will help you develop your intuitive ability with practice as recommended.

Hills, Christopher. "Opening the Intuition." Boulder Creek, CA: University of the Trees, 1979. Cassette tape starts with a chanting meditation followed by a discussion of what intuition is and how to develop it. Recommended for more advanced students of this subject.

"Learning to Think: Cassette Tape No. R–1051." Racine, WI: Johnson Foundation, 1984. Radio interview from Wingspread Conference Center with D. N. Perkins, author of *The Mind's Best Work*, and another researcher on some of the latest research in this field. Some of the discussion relates to intuition.

"Panel Discussion of Mobius Resource Psychics." Los Angeles: Mobius Society, March 30–31, 1985. Cassette tape of round table discussion by resource people Mobius uses on their applied research projects. Best part of tape is the description of different techniques and cues each employs to work on actual projects.

Puryear, Herbert B. "Enhance Your Psychic Potential: Tape Number 8." Virginia Beach: ARE Tapes, 1981. Cassette outlines steps to take to develop your psychic potential with emphasis on the spiritual level of your intuitive development.

Schwartz, Stephen. "Psi Q Test Which Appeared in Omni Magazine." Long Beach, CA: UMS Productions, 1983. Cassette taped interview from the television series "Quest Four" on his research on the use of brain styles and skills.

Targ, Russell, and Keith Harary. "Invitational Seminar in Extended Sensing: Presentation." Los Angeles: Mobius Society, March 30–31, 1985. Cassette tape of individual presentations by each researcher on the experiments they have been conducting on remote viewing or sensing.

Vaughan, Frances. "Awakening Intuition: *Psychology Today* Cassette Number 20272."

Washington, DC: American Psychological Association, 1982. Interview with the author of the book *Awakening Intuition*. Discusses what the skill is and some of the basic steps to developing your skill which parallel her book. Excellent and recommended.

————. "Exercises for Awakening the Intuitive You," *Psychology Today* Cassette Number 20273. Washington, DC: American Psychological Association, 1982. Follows the tape above with an actual work session on how to develop your skills. Excellent and recommended.

Wolf, Fred Alan. "The Quantum Factor: Cassette Tape Number 1930." San Francisco: New Dimensions Radio, 1985. Discusses how the mind works and in part how quantum physics can be directly related to the intuitive process.

B. Tests and Measurements of Intuition

There are a number of tests and instruments that can be used to measure intuition as defined above. Some are more traditionally recognized methods, while others are less formally recognized. Examples of both are cited for your own review and consideration.

Books and Monographs

Agor, Weston H. *Intuitive Management: Integrating Left and Right Brain Management Skills*. Englewood Cliffs, NJ: Prentice-Hall, 1984. Contains a test for intuitive ability as well as a description of how to use the results in applied management settings.

Brenner, Elizabeth. *Hand in Hand: Awareness and Compatibility—It's in Your Hands*. Millbrae, CA: Celestial Arts, 1981. Characteristics derived by professional palm reading.

Ebon, Martin, ed. *Test Your ESP*. New York: New American Library, 1970. Real life tests and exercises to measure this aspect of your intuitive ability.

Eysenck, Hans J., and Carl Sargent. *Know Your Own Psi-Q*. New York: World Almanac Publications, 1983. Primary use of this book is for the discussion of various techniques that can be used to measure the different levels of intuitive ability you may have.

Leibel, Charlotte P. *Change Your Handwriting, Change Your Life*. New York: Stein & Day, 1972. Explains how handwriting can be used to test your intuitive ability as well as other characteristics and to change yourself as well. See particularly the chapter on intuition and imagination. Because this person also has a strong formal training in the fields of law and psychology, her own capability of interpretation shows how this approach can be effectively used.

Loye, David. *The Knowable Future: A Psychology of Forecasting and Prophecy*. New York: John Wiley & Sons, 1978. Test measures are included and described for measuring precognitive ability.

————. *The Sphinx and the Rainbow: Brain, Mind and Future Vision*. Boulder, CO: Shambhla, 1983. Contains among many other things a good discussion on using intuitive brain skills for forecasting (precognition) and includes his HCP Profile Test which seeks to measure brain styles and relate them to precognitive forecasting ability.

Myers, Isabel Briggs. *The Myers–Briggs Type Indicator: 1962 Manual*. Palo Alto, CA:

Consulting Psychologists Press, 1962. Explains the Myers–Briggs Type Indicator, how it works, and how it can be interpreted, as well as other statistical support information on its use by organizations.

———. *Introduction to Type*. Palo Alto, CA: Consulting Psychologists Press, 1980. Explains characteristics and likely behavior based on your type after taking the Myers–Briggs Personality Test. The section on intuition is particularly useful, but so are other descriptions.

Taggert, William. *Administrators Manual for the Human Information Processing™ Survey and Strategy and Tactics Profile*. Bensonville, IL: Scholastic Testing Service, 1983. Describes how to interpret and use the results of the Human Information™ Survey. Also discusses the reliability and validity of the survey instrument. This instrument measures brain styles and classifies them in terms of left, right, mixed, and integrative.

Articles

Agor, Weston H. "Brain Skills Development in Management Training." *Training and Development Journal* 37, 4 (April 1983), pp. 78–83. Describes test and findings that measured intuitive ability, and also how to measure various brain skills on-the-job to increase productivity.

"The Eyes Have It When Interviewing Suspects." *Public Administration Times* (April 15, 1983), p. 12. Research of Dr. Dale G. Leathers at the University of Georgia shows which nonverbal cues mean what as contrasted with actual verbal statements being made by a respondent.

Herrmann, Ned. "The Brain and Management Learning." *Bureaucrat* (Fall 1982), pp. 17–21. Discusses his brain research and relates the findings to how to teach different management brain types most effectively.

Lee, Joyce. "You Can Raise Your IQ, Increase Your Self-Esteem, Create Energy, Improve Your Memory and Much Much More—With Graphotherapy." *New Woman Magazine* (July 1982), pp. 20–24. Discusses in popularized form Charlotte Leibel's book contents above.

Loye, David. "Foresight Saga." *Omni* (September 1982), pp. 20, 134. Summarizes his research as outlined in the books above.

McRae, Ronald W. "Psychic Warriors: Forget Death Rays and the Bomb. Psi Is the Weapon of the Future." *Omni* (April 1984), pp. 58–63, 126–27. Discusses military uses of psi in the United States and Russia.

Schkade, Lawrence L., and Alfred R. Potvin. "Cognitive Style, EEG Waveforms, and Brain Levels." *Human Systems Management Journal* (1981), pp. 329–31. Uses Herrmann Learning Profile Survey Form and applies electroencephalographic tests to selected subjects. Finds that it "validates" the Herrmann test. Recent brain research since would seriously question this conclusion.

Schwartz, Stephen A., and Rand De Mattei. "Psi-Q I Report." *Omni* (November 1982), pp. 24, 160–61. Summarizes the results of their national testing of over 18,000 *Omni* readers who took their test that measures precognitive ability as well as brain styles in 1981–82.

Tucker, Carll. "I Got My Job Through Human Engineering." *Village Voice* (November 3, 1975), reprint. Describes aptitude measurement program by the Johnson O'Connor Research Foundation.

"Two Houston Psychologists Are Proving the Best Defense Is Picking a Good Jury." *People* (February 1983), pp. 88–90. Intuition is used to pick juries.

Vivian, Eleanor L. "Personality Can Be 'Seen' in Graphic Evaluation Chart." *Journal of Graphoanalysis* (January 1983), p. 7. Describes how graphoanalysis can be professionally used to measure traits and characteristics including intuition.

Test Instruments

Agor, Weston H. *AIM Survey: Trainer's Guide*. Bryn Mawr, PA: Organization Design and Development, 1985. Prepared for organizational trainers and related personnel. Designed so that a person can use/administer the *AIM Survey* for more productive human capital management in a wide variety of situations and settings.

———. "Test Your Management Style and Response Form." Published in Weston H. Agor, *Intuitive Management: Integrating Left and Right Brain Management Skills* (Englewood Cliffs, NJ: Prentice-Hall, 1984). This test is based on selected questions from the intuition portion of the MBTI and the brain styles portion of the *Human Information*™ *Survey*. Measures underlying potential to use intuition as well as gives an indication of whether it is actually being used on-the-job to make decisions. The response form displays graphically what your test results are and what they mean/how they can be used applied to management situations.

———. *Test Your Intuitive Powers: AIM Survey*. Bryn Mawr, PA: Organization Design and Development, 1985. This instrument has two parts. The first part surveys your underlying intuitive ability and the second part measures how you use this brain skill on-the-job to make important decisions.

Briggs, Katherine C., and Isabel Briggs Myers. *Myers–Briggs Type Indicator—Form F*. Palo Alto, CA: Consulting Psychologists Press, 1976. Test that can be used to measure aspects of your personality including intuition. It is considered to be highly reliable and valid in the field of psychology, although there are those who believe that pen and pencil tests cannot effectively be used to measure actual expected behavior.

Fisher, Milton. "How Intuitive Are You?" *New Woman Magazine* (May 1982), pp. 42–44, 46. Includes test from Fisher's book above. This is a popularized test instrument and probably should not be used other than for fun as a guide. Rely on the other tests noted here for this purpose.

Goldberg, Philip. "Are You Intuitive?" A short test contained in Goldberg's book listed above. It is a popularized test instrument and probably should not be used other than for fun as a guide. Rely on other tests noted here for this purpose.

"Herrmann Participant Survey Form." Lake Lure, NC: Whole Brain Corporation, 1984. Survey instrument designed to show brain style preference. Can be used to help guide training program more effectively.

Loye, David. "Manual for the HCP Profile Test." Carmel, CA: Institute for Futures Forecasting, 1982. Seeks to measure brain styles and relationship to ability to forecast the future.

———. "The 1983 Knowable Future Study." Carmel, CA: Institute for Futures Forecasting, 1983. Seeks to measure brain styles and relationship to ability to forecast events in the immediate future.

Schwartz, Stephen A., and Rand De Mattei. "Mobius Psi-Q Test." *Omni* (October 1981), pp. 136–38, 159–60. Contains a test of both precognitive ability and also brain styles on-the-job with stratification for other factors such as sex and occupational specialty.

————. "Psi-Q Test II: Remote Viewing." *Omni* (October 1982), pp. 134–42, 182. Attempt to measure ability to see distant scenes or events using psychic powers alone (remote viewing). Experimental and innovative work.

————. "Mobius Psi-Q Test III." Unpublished. Current experimental questionnaire used by authors to attempt to link personality profiles with high intuitive functioning— especially remote viewing.

Singer, June, and Mary Loomis. *The Singer–Loomis Inventory of Personality*. Palo Alto, CA: Consulting Psychologists Press, 1984. This is a survey instrument which seeks to go beyond the MBTI by demonstrating that characteristics and abilities such as intuitive styles can be situational. Hence, in some cases we might practice a thinking style and in others an intuitive style depending on the situation. This has implications for use in situational leadership training and management.

Torrance, E. Paul, with Barbara and William Taggart. *Human Information*™ *Survey*. Bensonville, IL: Scholastic Testing Service, 1983. Surveys how a person processes information, and classifies the results into left, right, mixed, and integrated processor. Right processors prefer intuitive approaches to problems and decision making.

Vaughan, Alan. "The Psychic Defender." Software computer game developed for use on the Apple microcomputer. Enables you to practice and develop your intuitive skills.

C. Profiles of Intuitive Executives

Books

Bennis, Warren, and Burt Nanus. *Leaders: The Strategies for Taking Charge*. New York: Harper & Row, 1985. Points out that management training across the country today leaves out leadership training. An important part of that is the creative or intuitive process itself. Based on interviews with ninety successful CEOs who reveal the skills of an effective leader.

De Bono, Edward. *Tactics: The Art and Science of Success*. Boston: Little, Brown, 1984. The author analyzes interviews with prominent people to determine the secrets of their success. Intuition is one.

Kanter, Rosabeth Moss. *The Change Masters: Innovation for Productivity in the American Corporation*. New York: Simon & Schuster, 1983. One of the characteristics of an intuitive executive is that they are change masters.

Manchester, William. *The Last Lion: Winston Spencer Churchill*. New York: Dell, 1984. One of the interesting aspects of this book is the description of Churchill as an extroverted intuitive, and the characteristics this implies regarding his skills and also shortcomings in decision making.

Naisbitt, John, and Patricia Aburdene. *Reinventing the Corporation*. New York: Warner Books, 1985. One of the trends they see is the importance of intuition in the management of the corporations of the future.

Pinchott, Gifford, III. *Intrapreneuring*. New York: Harper & Row, 1985. He points out that the entrapreneur is highly intuitive and also integrative.

Rowan Roy. *The Intuitive Manager*. Boston: Little, Brown, 1986. Discusses the importance of intuitive ability in management based on extensive personal interviews with top executives over the last twenty years while serving on the Board of Editors of *Fortune*.

Zdenek, Marilee. *The Right-Brain Experience: An Intimate Program to Free the Powers of Your Imagination*. New York: McGraw-Hill, 1983. Features interviews with successful persons in a wide range of occupations revealing how they use their intuitive ability in their professional work.

Articles

Agor, Weston H. "The Logic of Intuition: How Successful Executives Make Important Decisions." *Organizational Dynamics* (Winter 1986), pp. 5–18. Discusses in much greater detail with extensive quotes the way top executives use their intuition to make important decisions.

Barger, Melvin D. "A Self-Starter Transforms General Motors." *Wall Street Journal* (August 24, 1983), p. 20. This book review of Charles Kettering, General Motors' legendary wizard of research, is worth reading in order to grasp the strengths and limitations of an intuitive executive type.

Benz, Jill. "Peak Performance." *New Realities* 5, 1 (December 1982), pp. 38–40. Discusses Dr. Charles A. Garfield's research on peak performance. Intuitive processes are among top executive's competencies.

Bittner, Sam. "Liberal Arts Majors Prove Specialization Isn't Required for Success in Business." *Chronicle of Higher Education* (April 14, 1982), p. 25. How intuition can be used to recruit successfully in spite of apparent facts.

Bolen, James Grayson. "Interview: Al Pollard." *Psychic* (December 1974), pp. 12–18, 56. Successful businessman tells how he views extrasensory perception and uses intuition in business.

Broad, William J. "Tracing the Skeins of Matter." *New York Times "Creative" Mind Series* (July 1984), reprint. This article is about Dr. Peter A. Carruthers, head of the theoretical division at the Los Alamos National Laboratory. He is a classic example of a highly intuitive thinker. Recommended reading especially for thinking style thinkers to reflect on.

Byrne, Harlan S. "New Chairman at Santa Fe Industries Using Risky Style of Leadership to Push Company." *Wall Street Journal* (September 11, 1983), p. 21. The CEO of this company describes how he makes sure his intuitive processes are free to flow for applied decision making.

Cole, Robert J. "Masters of the Corporate Turnaround." *New York Times* (July 31, 1983), section 3, pp. 1ff. Good personal profiles of how these executives have an intuitive sense of what to do.

———. "Telling Pickens That It Won't Be Easy." *New York Times* (November 6, 1983), p. F6. James E. Lee, chairman of Gulf Oil Corporation, uses spiritual meditation practices before making management decisions.

Dolan, Carrie. "A Bit of Old-Style Imagination Leads to a High-Tech Success." *Wall Street Journal* (February 21, 1983), p. 1. Describes how she went from a twenty-nine-year-old mother of two to a business with $10 million in sales.

Glave, Judie. "Anne Klein Team Splits Amiably." Associated Press Wire Service (December 20, 1984). Good example of how two intuitive executives communicate on a mental level for business success.

"Going for It: Who Are Today's New Magnates, New Moguls, New Wheeler-Dealers,

New Builders of Business Empires: Well, They're Women." *Southwest Airline Magazine* (June 1983), pp. 75ff. Discusses the success of a number of up and coming women executives from the Southwest. They have "new age" characteristics in common—a vision, a philosophy of life and work that governs their every move. They are all creative, and have found new solutions to old problems.

Goleman, Daniel. "Successful Executives Rely on Own Kind of Intelligence." *New York Times* (July 31, 1984), pp. Cl, 11. One of their intelligence tools is intuition. The article shows the style of thinking is tied to success.

Goodspeed, Bennett W. "Different Style of Analysis Imperative to Business: More Often Than Not, Intuition, Not Numbers, Tells the Real Story." *American Banker* (November 9, 1981), reprint. Late partner of Inferential Focus of New York tells why intuition counts and when.

Grey, Marilyn. "Creative Thinking." *Public Management* (February 1983), pp. 10–15. This psychologist tells the International City Managers Association how to think intuitively and why.

Hammonds, Keith H. "Innovation That Crosses Cultural Lines." *New York Times* (January 22, 1984), p. F17. Discusses a major study that shows innovation is directly linked to intuition.

Hayes, Thomas C. "Celestial Seasonings Pins Its Hopes on More Than Herbal Tea." *New York Times* (April 3, 1983), pp. 6–7. Tells how the cofounder of this firm feels he can succeed employing a higher level of consciousness than has often been characteristic of business.

Howe, Arthur. "Entrepreneurial Profiles." *American Way* (July 1984), pp. 51–54. Outlines a recent study of one hundred executives by McKinsey & Co. Intuitive thinking styles characterize the most successful.

"Iacocca: An Autobiography." *Newsweek* (October 8, 1984), pp. 50–71. One of the decision making skills that Iacocca identifies is the ability to use intuition.

"Inventive Genius Is Alive and Well in the U.S." *U.S. News and World Report* (June 13, 1983), pp. 61–63. Several profiles of intuitive inventors and how they think.

Isenberg, Daniel J. "How Senior Managers Think." *Harvard Business Review* (November–December 1984), pp. 81–90. His study of senior managers finds that the higher you go in a company, the more important it is that you combine intuition with so-called rationality in the decision making process.

King, Wayne. "Trammel Crow Comes to Town." *New York Times* (November 6, 1983), p. F4. An example of an intuitive executive who tries to guide his conduct with spiritual principles.

Kiracofe, John H. "Creative Thinking and the Problem-Solving Process." *Michigan Municipal League* (July 1984), pp. 130–32. An intuitive executive himself, this city manager of Berkley, Michigan, tells how to implement an integrated intuitive management program. Recommended reading.

Kleinfield, N. R. "Gentle Persistence Pays Off: Top Headhunters Lester Korn and Richard Ferry." *New York Times* (October 30, 1983), pp. F6–7. A good example of two major executives who communicate on a mental level intuitively.

Kreskin. "How to Make Decisions." *Kiwanis Magazine* (March 1984), pp. 21–23. This famous mentalist discusses integrating both left and right brain techniques to make the best decision.

Larson, Erik. "Did Psychic Powers Give Firm a Killing in the Silver Market?" *Wall Street Journal* (December 6, 1984), p. 1. Describes efforts by Delphi Associates of San Mateo, California (Russell Targ and Keith Harary), to apply psychic skills to business decision making with mixed success.

Lasden, Martin. "Intuition: The Voice of Success?" *Computer Decisions* (February 26, 1985), pp. 98–104. Discusses how several successful executives in the computer field use intuition to guide their decisions.

Levitt, Arthur J., Jr., and Jack Albertine. "The Successful Entrepreneur: A Personality Profile." *Wall Street Journal* (August 29, 1983), p. 12. Says success is linked to a style that encourages experimentation not bureaucracy, informality rather than highly structured environments, and willingness to take risks.

Mahon, Gigi. "The Rothschild Touch: How Top Money Manager Madelon Talley Manages Money." *Barron's* (December 12, 1983), pp. 11, 30–33. An interview with a successful investment banker on Wall Street who is highly intuitive. Reading this interview will give you a good sense of how she integrates both intuitive and thinking type cues.

———. "Sweet Smell of Success: Meet Cosmetic Executive Lindsay Owen-Jones." *Barron's* (December 5, 1983), pp. 30–34. Profile of the CEO of Estee Lauder who believes intuition is critical to success in this industry.

Nemy, Enid. "May Sarton: Creative Solitude at 71." *New York Times* (November 20, 1983), p. Y42. Profile of a famous intuitive writer who appears to be an introverted type. Her views are worth reading.

———. "Women and Investment: An Expert Says They Are Too Fearful of Risks." *New York Times* (December 18, 1983), p. Y44. Profile of an intuitive executive, Julia Walsh, who heads an investment firm in Washington, DC. She is a risk taker.

"The Right Stuff." *Forbes* (December 17, 1984), p. 10. Tells about a firm, Perception International, that uses intuitive techniques to serve clients.

Robinson, Jeffrey. "Blooming Genius: Inventor Clive Sinclair Strikes It Rich." *Barron's* (December 12, 1983), pp. 14, 36. A profile of an intuitive executive in the computer industry. His views on innovation are worth reading carefully.

Shellenbarger, Sue. "Quaker Oats Chairman to Continue to Make Changes in New Position." *Wall Street Journal* (November 11, 1984), pp. 25, 39. Profile of another intuitive executive who promotes risk taking.

Siebert, Al. "The Survivor Personality." *Portland Oregonian Northwest Magazine* (January 27, 1980), Reprint. Based on extensive interviews with successful executives, the author concludes intuitive ability is a common trait these entrepreneurs have.

Sugg, John. "Making the Leap—Successful Entrepreneurs and Executives Trust Their Hunches—and It Pays Off." *Working Women* (November 1982), pp. 38–42. Successful use of intuition in business is outlined.

Sullivan, Michael P. "The Intuitive Approach Is Making a Quiet Comeback." *American Banker* (March 16, 1983), p. 4. Banks like intuition these days.

Wayne, Leslie. "A Pioneer Spirit Sweeps Business." *New York Times* (March 25, 1984), section 3, pp. 1ff. Characteristics of the new entrepreneur in business. One is intuitive ability.

Wills, Kendall J. "An Explorer Charts the Passages of the Executive Mind." *New York*

Times (March 6, 1983), p. D1. Efforts to chart how top executives think by Abraham Zaleznik at Harvard Business School.

II. IMPLEMENTING A PROGRAM TO USE AND DEVELOP INTUITION TO INCREASE PRODUCTIVITY IN YOUR ORGANIZATION

This section is divided into two major parts. The first part includes references to the dangers of failing to integrate intuitive brain skills into daily decision making in organizations today. The second part contains citations to sources that explain how to go about developing your intuitive skills, and how to integrate them into the decision making process to help increase productivity—both on a personal and on an organizational level.

A. Dangers of Failing to Integrate Intuitive Brain Skills into Organizational Decision Making

Books

Allison, Graham T. *Essence of Decision: Explaining the Cuban Missile Crisis.* Boston: Little, Brown, 1971. Author examines the Cuban missile crisis, and demonstrates different thinking styles and routines that can affect the outcome of a decision. Clearly shows the importance of integrating different brain styles into the final product.

Integrity in the College Curriculum: A Report to the Academic Community. Washington, DC: Association of American Colleges, February 1985. Calls for as one recommendation a minimum college curriculum that teaches the legitimacy of intuition in thinking and critical analysis.

Starling, Grover. *Managing the Public Sector.* Homewood, IL: Dorsey Press, 1986. Chapters on decision making show the dangers of "group think" discussed in this book.

Articles

"Atari Story Shows Lack of Balance." United Press International Wire Service (September 26, 1984). This story shows clearly the importance of integrating intuitive and thinking brain skills in management. Blind spots develop if you do not, as in this case example.

Bennett, Robert A. "Bank America in Search of Itself." *New York Times* (October 30, 1983), pp. F7, and F9. In the context of the rapidly changing banking business, this article discusses the difficulties this bank is having anticipating change and adapting to it. One of the primary factors is the thinking styles of the business executives themselves.

Bleakley, Fred R. "Behind the Big Collapse at Osborne." *New York Times* (November 6, 1983), pp. F1, 26. This is an excellent case study of factors that can be allowed to get in the way of the natural intuitive flow in decision making, resulting in major business failure. Worth careful study.

Broad, William J. "The Science Corps Wants a Few More Good Heretics." *New York Times* (October 16, 1983), p. EY8. This is an excellent article to read to get a "feel" for the tension between intuitive thinking and bureaucratic thinking styles. The former in this case led to a Nobel Prize and the latter to maintaining the status quo.

Cox, Meg. "Ex-Chief of Recovering AM International Appears to Be a Victim of His Own Success." *Wall Street Journal* (January 27, 1984), p. 25. This is an excellent personal example of how an individual's thinking management style is often not balanced by corresponding intuitive skills, resulting in major blind spots that can cause failure unless steps are taken to compensate for them. The reverse is equally true. The key is to integrate both brain skills in management.

Dunne, John Gregory. "Bureaucrats in Blue." *New York Times Book Review* (November 6, 1983), p. 9. This book review shows how brain types tend to select particular occupation specialties—in this case thinking style with the New York Police Department.

Harris, Kathryn. "Disney Lays the Groundwork for Its Voyage to Tomorrowland." *Los Angeles Times* (June 27, 1982), business section, p. 1. What has happened since the departure of intuitive Walt Disney is explained.

"Harvard's Bok Urges Changing 'Expensive, Inefficient' Legal System, Seeks Law-School Curriculum Reform." *Chronicle of Higher Education* (May 4, 1983), pp. 8–9. Asks legal educators to take a more integrated view of what they should be delivering in the way of a model for tomorrow's needs.

Keller, Evelyn Fox. "Contending with a Masculine Bias in the Ideals and Values of Science." *Chronicle of Higher Education* (October 2, 1985), p. 96. Demonstrates how male dominant thinking style researchers promoted "thinking scientifically meant thinking like a man." This means reason and feelings somehow cannot go together in science. She argues for integrating the workplace, which is the same as integrating thinking and intuitive brain skills.

Koten, John. "GM–Toyota Venture Stirs Major Antitrust and Labor Problems." *Wall Street Journal* (June 10, 1983), pp. 1, 14. Discusses some of the practical problems involved in this joint venture effort, and attempts to overcome them.

Kristol, Irving. "Put Not Your Faith in Economic Soothsayers." *Wall Street Journal* (August 30, 1983), p. 17. Thinking style economic forecasts of the future are often wrong. This article explains why. It also demonstrates once again the importance of integrating brain skills for decision making.

Langley, Monica. "AT&T Marketing Men Find Their Star Fails to Ascend as Expected." *Wall Street Journal* (February 13, 1984), pp. 1, 19. This article shows how the clash of brain styles can affect corporate performance if not managed properly.

Le Franchi, Howard. "Futurist Toffler Calls for 'De-Massifying' of Schools." *Christian Science Monitor* (December 7, 1984), pp. 33, 36. Toffler clearly outlines ways in which we can move to integrate intuitive and thinking brain skills to prepare for the future that is emerging. Good piece to read for those wishing to organize and/or join intuition networks.

Lynch, Mitchell. "Polaroid Tries to Get Itself in Focus." *New York Times* (May 15, 1983), p. F4. Discusses the problems the company is having generating the level of creativity that characterized the company under the leadership of Edwin Land.

Magnuson, Robert. "Battered in 1981, Economic Forecasters Resolve to Do Better in 1982." *Los Angeles Times* (January 3, 1982), pp. 1, 4. Thinking style economic projections standing alone appear to be "off the wall" despite all the facts and all the computers.

Malabre, Alfred L., Jr. "If One Economist Goofs, Will 46 Do Any Better? Robert Eggert Thinks So, and He May Be Right." *Wall Street Journal* (April 6, 1983), p. 50. Consensus forecasting appears to work better than going it alone. Intuition and synergy at work.

McGinley, Laurie. "Forecasters Overhaul 'Models' of Economy in Wake of 1982 Errors." *Wall Street Journal* (February 17, 1983), pp. 1, 20. Despite thinking style forecasters' promises to do better in 1982, they did not. This should help demonstrate the importance of intuition in decision making.

Navrozov, Lev. "Why the CIA Undershoots Soviet Arms Spending." *Wall Street Journal* (December 6, 1983), p. 28. Shows how closed, highly structured bureaucracies often work to shut off the intuitive process. The result affects performance.

Nelson, Bryce. "Management 'Revolution' Urged for Auto Industry." *Los Angeles Times* (July 27, 1982), pp. 1 and 15. Discusses the need for integrated thinking in the auto industry. Since this article was written, General Motors in particular has taken several steps in this direction.

Nichols, David A. "Can 'Theory Z' Be Applied to Academic Management?" *Chronicle of Higher Education* (September 1, 1982), p. 72. Going to the East for answers in our higher education system is his suggestion.

Norris, Floyd. "Bear with Us: Three Errant Seers Tell Where They Went Wrong." *Barron's* (February 13, 1984), pp. 8–9. This article clearly shows that understanding the stock market requires more than simply thinking style skills and analysis.

Palmer, Brad. "Does MBA Stand for Missing Business Acumen?" *Wall Street Journal* (December 28, 1983), p. 13. Argues that success in business requires the ability to effectively work with people and an uncertain world more than technical expertise emphasized in most MBA programs.

Rose, Frank. "The Mass Production of Engineers: The Future Is Being Designed by Engineers. The One Thing We Know About the Future Is That It's More Complicated Than That." *Esquire* (May 1983), pp. 74–84. Discusses the need to change the way we are training our engineers, to have judgment as well as technical expertise.

Schlesinger, James R. "Reorganizing the Joint Chiefs." *Wall Street Journal* (February 8, 1984), p. 28. This article by the former secretary of defense shows clearly the limitations of thinking management styles standing alone, and the need to integrate them with intuitive brain styles—particularly in crisis settings.

Seib, Kenneth. "How the Laws of Academics Work to Prevent Change." *Chronicle of Higher Education* (January 25, 1984), point of view section, p. 64. A classic description of how thinking style bureaucratic routines thwart intuitive processes in higher education.

"Strength of the Dollar Is Explained by a Mix of Economics, Psychology." *Wall Street Journal* (December 14, 1983), pp. 29 and 41. This article shows clearly that understanding trends requires integrating both thinking and intuitive brain skills. In this case, the dollar was not going in the direction the "facts" standing alone said it should.

Tyrrell, R. Emmett, Jr. "Recovery Unutterable for Economic 'Gurus'." *Sun–Sentinel* (March 11, 1983), p. 19. We often pay more for thinking style economic projections than they are worth.

"Visions: Report on Cal State's Future Raises Doubts." *Los Angeles Times* (February

6, 1983), pp. 1, 22. Among other things, this report acknowledges that intuition—particularly extrasensory perception—may be taught effectively and that we should consider this fact in our school systems.

Wallace, Anise C. "Why Money Managers Bombed." *New York Times* (January 22, 1984), p. F4. Predicting the future, this article shows, requires intuitive as well as thinking skills.

Watkins, Beverly T. "Business Schools Told They Should Produce Generalists, Not Specialists." *Chronicle of Higher Education* (April 25, 1984), p. 13. The CEOs of top American companies and the deans and alumni of prestigious business schools conclude in a recent study that an "ideal" graduate program should produce generalists—managers with a broad educational background and a sound grounding in ethics—rather than specialists to fill positions in business today.

———— "Other Fields Can Yield Business Professors, Dean Says." *Chronicle of Higher Education* (May 9, 1984), p. 14. Argues that business schools might well improve their programs by overcoming the narrow view of what constitutes a qualified faculty member.

"Why Cynicism Can Be Fatal." *Newsweek* (September 10, 1984), p. 68. Research shows that cynics are least likely to be intuitive. This article explains why.

Winkler, Karen J. "Questioning the Science in Social Science, Scholars Signal a Turn to Interpretation." *Chronicle of Higher Education* (June 26, 1985), pp. 5–6. Calls for interdisciplinary research which includes personal interpretation like that called for here in Chapter 7 regarding research on intuition.

"The World's Smartest Man Revisited." *Inferential Focus Report* (April 11, 1983), pp. 1–4. Examines former Soviet Leader Andropov from an intuitive brain perspective. The conclusion: He was a thinking style leader. It is interesting to note the style of the new Soviet leader in contrast. It would appear that the new leadership has a greater capacity to use and value intuitive skills.

Young, John A. "One Company's Quest for Improved Quality." *Wall Street Journal* (July 25, 1983), p. 10. Describes quality improvement efforts at Hewlett–Packard Co. Written by the president, one key factor found would appear to be intuitive management.

B. How to Develop and Integrate Intuition into Individual and Organizational Decision Making Processes

Books

Agor, Weston H. *Intuitive Management: Integrating Left and Right Brain Management Skills*. Englewood Cliffs, NJ: Prentice-Hall, 1984. Discusses in detail how to integrate intuition into management decision making in an applied way, using numerous real life organizational examples.

Albrecht, Karl. *Brain Power: Learn to Improve Your Thinking Skills*. Englewood Cliffs, NJ: Prentice-Hall, 1980. A practical guide with exercises on how to improve your brain skills in an integrated way.

Ascher, William. *Forecasting: An Appraisal for Policy-Makers and Planners*. Baltimore: Johns Hopkins University Press, 1978. Discusses different types of forecasting including the use of intuition as a particular application.

Blum, Ralph. *The Book of Runes*. New York: St. Martin's Press, 1982. Western world version of I Ching. It is a useful instrument for projection and analysis. Contains twenty-five ceramic stones and book to interpret their meaning.

Blumberg, Stephen K. *Win–Win Administration: How to Manage an Organization So Everybody Wins.* Sun Lakes, AZ: Thomas Horton and Daughters, 1983. Example of the move to more cooperative styles of management where intuitive skills will be most useful.

Bro, Harmon H. *Edgar Cayce on Dreams.* New York: Warner Books, 1968. Through this intuitive's eyes, advice on how to use your dreams as a tool to get in touch with your intuition.

Buzan, Tony. *Use Both Sides of Your Brain.* New York: E. P. Dutton, 1983. As the title suggests, integrative use of the brain is most productive. The technique of mind mapping is discussed for improving learning.

Carskadon, Thomas G., ed. *Research in Psychological Type: Volumes 5 and 6.* Mississippi State: Mississippi State University, 1982 and 1983. Outlines in a series of articles the practical application of MBTI results to various organizational settings and problems including cross-cultural ones.

De A'Morelli, Richard. *ESP Party Games: Psychic Tests for Everyone.* Chatsworth, CA: Major Books, 1979. Games you can play to work on developing your intuitive ability.

De Bono, Edward. *New Think: The Use of Lateral Thinking in the Generation of New Ideas.* New York: Avon, 1985. Author defines ways of thinking that are unorthodox and can lead to solutions to intractable problems. Intuition is a critical brain skill in this process.

Denhardt, Robert B. *Theories of Public Organization.* Monterey, CA: Brooks/Cole, 1984. Outlines the major theories concerning how the public sector should be organized. You cannot do it without the use of intuition.

Edwards, Betty. *Drawing on the Right Side of the Brain.* Los Angeles: J. P. Tarcher, 1979. How to draw even if you have never been an artist. Tells you how to tap into the right side of the brain to do so. This technique or others like it is one way to develop your intuition. See chapter on Zen in drawing in particular.

Eysenck, H. J., and Leon Kamin. *The Intelligence Controversy.* New York: John Wiley & Sons, 1981. Discusses the recent controversy over the validity of intelligence tests. More recent work by Howard Gardner at Harvard is a breakthrough in this regard.

Ferguson, Marilyn. *The Aquarian Conspiracy: Personal and Social Transformation in the 1980's.* Los Angeles: J. P. Tarcher, 1980. Shows how intuitive approaches are transforming the way we manage all types of organizations and our personal life as well.

Flory, Charles D. *Managing Through Insight.* New York: Mentor Paperback, 1968. Discusses the practical use of intuitive skills in management decision making.

Gardner, Howard. *Frames of Mind: The Theory of Multiple Intelligences.* New York: Basic Books, 1983. Discusses his theory of multiple intelligences. Chapter on personal intelligences is probably most relevant to intuitive applications in management.

Gardner, Martin. *Aha! Insight.* New York: Scientific American, 1978. Problems to work on to develop your intuitive skills.

Girdano, Daniel, and George Everly. *Controlling Stress and Tension: A Holistic Approach.* Englewood Cliffs, NJ: Prentice-Hall, 1979. Shows how important stress management is. Learning to follow your intuition will help you to reduce stress and manage better.

Gittner, Louis. *Listen, Listen, Listen: Opens the Door to Spiritual Transformation*. Orcas Island, WA: Louis Foundation, 1980. Type of book to read when you need philosophical food to alter or consider altering your present way of thinking.

Hamachek, Don E. *Encounters with Others: Interpersonal Relationships and You*. New York: Holt, Rinehart & Winston, 1982. Ways to establish and maintain good relationships. Useful for team building in organizations.

Harvard Business Review. *On Human Relations*. New York: Harper & Row, 1979. Focuses on "right brain" aspects of management, including a section on intuitive ways of relating to people.

Herzog, Stephanie. *Joy in the Classroom*. Boulder Creek, CA: University of the Trees Press, 1982. Teaching meditation and other techniques at the primary and secondary school level. I have been to their school and the energy the students have is incredible. I recommend every school district look at what they have to offer.

Hills, Christopher. *Creative Conflict: Learning to Love with Total Honesty*. Boulder Creek, CA: University of the Trees Press, 1980. Learning to manage conflict by first getting in touch with yourself.

———. *Into Meditation Now: A Course on Direct Enlightenment*. Boulder Creek, CA: University of the Trees Press, 1979. Introduction to meditation techniques, which can be followed up by other materials that they have available for further development.

Hills, Christopher, and Deborah Rozman. *Exploring Inner Space: Awareness Games for All Ages*. Boulder Creek, CA: University of the Trees Press, 1978. How to get in touch with your own self and, thereby, everybody else.

Hills, Norah. *You Are a Rainbow*. Boulder Creek, CA: University of the Trees Press, 1979. Discusses aura levels and aura balancing.

Houston, Jean. *The Possible Human: A Course in Enhancing Your Physical, Mental, and Creative Abilities*. Los Angeles: J. P. Tarcher, 1982. Teaches you some of the ways to get in touch with yourself and tap your intuitive ability.

Howell, William S. *The Empathic Communicator*. Belmont, CA: Wadsworth, 1982. Discusses the importance of empathy in organizational communication. Several examples of the use and importance of intuition are included.

Jampolsky, Gerald G. *Love Is Letting Go of Fear*. New York: Bantam Books, 1981. One of the keys to developing your intuition is developing the capacity to give up the past when necessary. This tells you how.

Joy, W. Brugh. *Joy's Way: A Map for the Transformational Journey*. Los Angeles: J. P. Tarcher, 1979. Tells you how to develop your psi ability based on his experience as a doctor.

Keirsey, David, and Marilyn Bates. *Please Understand Me: An Essay on Temperament Styles*. Del Mar, CA: Prometheus Nemesis Books, 1978. Details how the Myers–Briggs personality types are likely to function in organizational settings and in their personal lives. Very useful to show you how to apply intuition scores to solve practical business problems.

Kivenson, Gilbert. *The Art and Science of Inventing*. New York: Van Nostrand Reinhold, 1982. Chapter 8 of this book concerns the psychology of invention, and relates the process of invention to fulfilling the inner needs of the inventor.

Krieger, Dolores. *The Therapeutic Touch: How to Use Your Hands to Help or to Heal*.

Englewood Cliffs, NJ: Prentice-Hall, 1979. A nurse, who has taught how we can heal ourselves and others, tells you how here.

Lawrence, Gordon. *People Types and Tiger Stripes: A Practical Guide to Learning Styles*, 2nd ed. Gainesville, FL: Center for Applications of Psychological Type, 1982. Takes the Myers–Briggs personality types, explains different learning styles, and gives exercises on how to alter your type (or develop it). Useful practically to show again how intuition can be used in a variety of organizational settings.

Litvak, Stuart B. *Use Your Head: How to Develop the Other 80% of Your Brain*. Englewood Cliffs, NJ: Prentice-Hall, 1982. Very useful book to help you get in touch with your real potential. Chapter on intuition is a good introduction. This might be a book to start with.

Lynch, Dudley. *Your High-Performance Business Brain: An Operator's Manual*. Englewood Cliffs, NJ: Prentice-Hall, 1984. Several of the chapters in this book are most useful for making you sensitive to the value of integrating opposites together somewhere in the process of business decision making.

Manning, Al G. *Helping Yourself with E.S.P*. West Nyack, NY: Parker, 1966. This person became a successful business executive. His focus is to help you develop your extrasensory perception.

Masters, Robert, and Jean Houston. *Mind Games: The Guide to Inner Space*. New York: Dell Books, 1972. A how-to book of mental exercises for achieving altered states of consciousness. Often called the yoga of the West.

Matlin, Margaret. *Cognition*. New York: Holt, Rinehart & Winston, 1983. Chapters on imagery, problem solving and creativity, reasoning, and decision making are useful.

May, Rollo. *The Courage to Create*. New York: Bantam Books, 1975. If you know how to be creative, you need to get in touch with your intuition. You need to be courageous to do either.

McCaulley, Mary H. *Executive Summary: Application of the Myers–Briggs Type Indicator to Medicine and Other Health Professions*. Gainesville, FL: Center for Applications of Psychological Type, 1978. Discusses how the MBTI can be used to guide career selection in the medical and other health professions as well as related matters such as patient care.

McCaulley, Mary H., E. S. Gooleski, Charles F. Yokomoto, Lee Harrisberger, and E. Dendy Sloan. *Applications of Psychological Type in Engineering Education*. Gainesville, FL: Center for Applications of Psychological Type, 1983. Discusses how the MBTI can be used to guide career selection and education in the field of engineering.

Musashi, Miyamoto. *The Book of Five Rings: The Real Art of Japanese Management*. New York: Bantam Books, 1982. Shows how inductive methods can be used to manage your organization and your life. Clearly intuition is one of those.

Myers, Isabel Briggs. *Type and Teamwork*. Gainesville, FL: Center for Applications of Psychological Type, 1974. Outlines how MBTI results can be used as a guide for effective team building and management in organizations of all types.

Myers, Isabel Briggs, and Peter B. Myers. *Gifts Differing*. Palo Alto, CA: Consulting Psychologists Press, 1980. Excellent practical guide on how to use the Myers–Briggs test to address all types of organizational problems. It shows also which occupations intuitive types are most likely to be effective in.

Naisbitt, John. *Megatrends: Ten New Directions Transforming Our Lives*. New York:

Warner Books, 1984. Discusses the ten trends he sees emerging that will affect our lives. Since the writing of the book, the author has identified the use of intuition in management as an emerging trend as well.

Ohmare, Kenichi. *The Mind of the Strategist: Business Planning for Competitive Advantage.* New York: Penguin Books, 1983. In strategic planning, intuitive skills are important to success.

Pascale, Richard Tanner, and Anthony G. Athos. *The Art of Japanese Management: Applications for American Executives.* New York: Warner Books, 1981. Key to inductive approaches and their application to management. Chapter 4 on Zen and the art of management is particularly relevant to showing how intuition can be applied to management settings.

Perkins, D. N. *The Mind's Best Work.* Cambridge, MA: Harvard University Press, 1981. Takes an integrative view of the use of intuition including many useful exercises.

Peters, Thomas J., and Robert H. Waterman, Jr. *In Search of Excellence: Lesson from America's Best-Run Companies.* New York: Harper & Row, 1982. Tells how America's best run companies function and finds that the traits correlated with those of a creative person are often associated with intuitive thinking.

Plovnick, Mark S., Ronald E. Fry, and W. Warner Burke. *Organization Development: Exercises, Cases, and Readings.* Boston: Little, Brown, 1982. Variety of readings on processes of organizational development.

Raudsepp, Eugene. *How Creative Are You?* New York: Perigee Books, 1981. The third in the series. Best to read this book and then use the other two for exercises since it gives you an overview and test of your creativity.

———. *More Creative Growth Games.* New York: Perigee Books, 1980. Second in the three part series of game books for the same purpose.

Raudsepp, Eugene, with George P. Hough, Jr. *Creative Growth Games.* New York: Perigee Books, 1977. Games to practice and develop your creativity. This requires an integration of both thinking and intuitive styles.

Rico, Gabriele Lusser. *Writing the Natural Way.* Los Angeles: J. P. Tarcher, 1983. Teaches how to use "right brain" techniques to release your expressive powers. Useful in, e.g., organizational settings such as copy writing and advertising.

Roberts, Jane. *How to Develop Your ESP Power.* New York: Frederick Fell, 1980. Another primer on intuitive ability.

Robey, Daniel. *Designing Organizations: A Macro Perspective.* Homewood, IL: Richard D. Irwin, 1982. A basic textbook on organizational theory and design in management. Chapter on organizations in the future shows why intuition will be an important management skill.

Rozman, Deborah. *Meditation for Children.* Milbrae, CA: Celestial Arts, 1976. Tells you how to meditate with your family, your children, and yourself. Great for us all.

Rubenstein, Moshe F., and Kenneth Pfeiffer. *Concepts in Problem Solving.* Englewood Cliffs, NJ: Prentice-Hall, 1980. A very good outline of how to problem-solve in an integrated way.

Sargent, Alice G. *The Androgynous Manager.* New York: AMACOM, 1981. Outlines in many ways how and why top managers need to be both intuitive and integrative to succeed.

Schemel, George J., and James A. Borbely. *Facing Your Type.* Wernersville, PA: Typofile Press, 1982. This is designed to complement the MBTI in understanding and interpreting your personality type and abilities, including intuition. A step for developing your intuition is understanding yourself.

Schon, Donald A. *The Reflective Practitioner—How Professionals Think in Action.* New York: Basic Books, 1983. Treats different types of professionals and how they think. The importance and use of intuition are discussed frequently.

Scott, Ian, ed. *The Luscher Color Test: The Remarkable Test That Reveals Your Personality Through Color.* New York: Pocket Books, 1969. Translated from the original German, this is an excellent deep psychological test that can be used both for diagnosis and also for developing one's intuitive ability. Based on your preference for basic colors and the order therein.

Steadman, Alice. *Who's the Matter with Me?* Marina del Rey, CA: DeVorss, 1969. Gives you a good understanding of the relationship between your health and your way of thinking.

Tageson, C. William. *Humanistic Psychology: A Synthesis.* Homewood, IL: Dorsey Press, 1982. Treats this subfield of psychology and the major theorists therein.

Thurston, Mark A. *Understand and Develop Your ESP.* Virginia Beach, VA: ARE Press, 1977. Development of your intuitive abilities following methods Edgar Cayce outlined for you.

Van Oech, Roger. *A Whack on the Side of the Head: How to Unlock Your Mind for Innovation.* New York: Warner Books, 1983. Names ten blocks to innovation and helps you to think your way around them. Excellent for applied use in organizations.

Weinstein, Matt, and Loel Goodman. *Playfair: Everybody's Guide to Noncompetitive Play.* San Luis Obispo, CA: Impact, 1980. A guide to the new age of noncompetitive games that can be used in workshops in various organizational settings.

Whitehead, Don. *The Dow Story: The History of the Dow Chemical Company.* New York: McGraw-Hill, 1968. Chronicles the changes at Dow from 1890 to 1968. Useful only to relate to the case study simulation in Chapter 5.

Wilhelm, Richard, and Cary F. Baynes. *The I Ching or Book of Changes.* Princeton, NJ: Princeton University Press, 1977. Projection instrument used together with coins that are tossed and interpreted by appropriate readings in the book.

Williams, Paul. *Das Energi.* New York: Electra Books, 1973. A book to read and reread periodically. It will help you understand you, everyone, and everything else. It will help you develop your intuition.

Zager, Robert, and Michael P. Rosow. *The Innovative Organization: Productivity Programs in Action.* Elmsford, NY: Pergamon Press, 1982. Shows how employee participation must, and will, increase in organizations if productivity is to be increased. Intuition will become more important as a skill of management in this process.

Articles

Agor, Weston H. "How to Make Your Intuition Work for You." *Bell Atlantic Journal* 2, 3 (September 1985), pp. 2–7. Discusses how intuition can be used at all levels by the Bell Atlantic Telephone Company to meet the challenge of rapid change now upon the telecommunications industry.

———. "Intuition: A Management Resource for Increasing Organizational Productivity." *Bottom Line* 3, 2 (Fall–Winter 1985), pp. 33–34, 57. Tells budget and finance managers how they can apply their intuition to improve their work.

—————. "Intuition as a Brain Skill in Health Care Management." *Journal of Health and Human Resources Administration* (Winter 1985), pp. 386–95. Shows how intuition can be used to improve health and human services management.

—————. "Intuition as a Brain Skill in Management." *Public Personnel Management* 14, 1 (1985), pp. 15–24. Outlines why intuition is an important management brain skill, and important to search for in personnel programs in government.

—————. "Intuition in School Management." *School Administrator* 41, 6 (June 1984), pp. 12–14. Explains how intuition can be used to manage school systems most effectively.

—————. "Management in the Future: Using Intuitive Thinking." *Real Estate Business* (Summer 1983), pp. 14–17, 27. Describes how using intuition to make management decisions will have particular relevance as a survival skill in the real estate industry.

—————. "Managing Brain Skills to Increase Productivity." *Public Administration Review* (November–December 1985), pp. 864–68. Discusses how techniques in Chapter 5 can be implemented in public organizations. Two case study examples are featured.

—————. "A Management Skill for the 1990's." *Training: The Magazine of Human Resource Development* (March 1985), pp. 105–6. Discusses the importance of and ways to use intuition in management.

—————. "Tomorrow's Intuitive Leaders." *Futurist* (August 1983), pp. 49–53. Outlines why intuition will be a premium management skill in the future and how to test for it, develop it, and use it to make decisions.

—————. "Training Public Managers to Develop and Use Their Intuition for Decision Making." In *Professional Development Handbook, 1983*, edited by Kent T. Higgins. Washington, DC: American Society for Public Administration, 1983. Reports results of nationally testing a random sample of public administrators and outlines how to develop intuitive ability through a training program using many of the materials outlined in this book.

—————. "Using Brain Skill Assessments to Increase Productivity in Development Administration." *Public Administration and Development* 4, 4 (October–December 1984), pp. 335–42. Shows how intuition can be used in an international context to solve problems most productively.

—————. "Using Intuition in Development Administration." *International Journal of Public Administration* 6, 4 (December 1984), pp. 471–79. Outlines applications of intuition in the management of developing countries and international organizations which include cross-cultural membership.

—————. "Using Intuition in Nursing Management." *Nursing Success Today* (October 1984), pp. 23–24. Tells how intuition can be used in specific situations to improve nursing management and decision making.

—————. "Using Intuition in Public Management." *Public Management* (February 1983), pp. 2–6. Reports on testing of over 2,000 managers nationally, and outlines how intuition can be used and trained for in public organizations.

—————. "Using Intuition to Improve State Government Productivity." *State Government* 57, 4 (December 1984), pp. 125–28. Discusses ways in which intuition can improve state government productivity.

—————. "Using Intuition to Manage Organizations." *Bureaucrat: The Journal for Public Managers* 12, 4 (Winter 1983–84), pp. 49–52. In a special issue on trends in public administration, this article explains how using intuition will be a particularly useful skill for coping with the future changes emerging.

———. "Using Intuition to Manage Organizations in the Future." *Business Horizons* (July 1984), pp. 49–54. This article points out that a successful top manager in the future will need to possess intuitive skills as well as analytical skills in order to survive successfully. It also argues for the implementation of training programs in intuitive skills in order to prepare managers for the future.

Allen, Steve. "For Better Care and Feeding of the Gifted." *New York Times* (November 13, 1983), section 12, pp. 68–69. One of our neglected resources is the gifted. Intuitive ability is linked to research on intelligence level. Put the two together, and you have a place to start working on developing this talent. The author argues as I do in this book that how you go about motivating an intuitive person can be one key to better performance.

Apear, Leonard M. "In Peer-Group Discussions Executives Lay Their Management Woes on the Table." *Wall Street Journal* (August 21, 1985), p. 25. Shows that the approaches recommended in Chapter 5 work to increase productivity.

"Are You Creative? Research Shows Creativity Can Be Taught—And Companies Are Listening." *Business Week* (September 30, 1985), pp. 80–84. How workshops are being used to teach creativity today in business. Some researchers like Herbert A. Simon believe we can explain how the creative process works step-by-step.

Armstrong, Ellen. "Putting Intuition to Work: How to Succeed in Business by Trusting Your Hunches." *New Age Journal* (December 1985), pp. 32–37, 81. Discusses some of the latest research and applied training being done in this field.

Baradat De Valle, Maria Elena. "La Intuicion: Explorando El Sexto Sentido." *Harpers Bazaar En Español* (June 1983), pp. 70–71, 103. Magazine interviews with me concerning my work and workshops on intuition conducted in Miami, Florida.

Bennis, Warren. "Leadership Transforms Vision into Action." *Industry Week* (May 31, 1982), pp. 54–56. Shows how integrating intuitive skills in decision making leads to visionary leadership.

Berg, Eric N. "Zen and the Stanford Business Student: Creativity Skills Are Taught by Way of I Ching and Chanting. But the Aim Is Serious " *New York Times* (January 30, 1983), p. 9. Describes the Ray and Myers creativity class previously noted.

Calonius, L. Erik. "Factory Magic: In a Plant in Memphis, Japanese Firm Shows How to Attain Quality." *Wall Street Journal* (April 29, 1983), pp. 1, 14. A supportive and cooperative environment emphasizing inductive as well as deductive techniques is discussed.

Cameron, Kim S., and David A. Whetten. "Teaching Management Skills." Reprinted from *Exchange: The Organizational Behavior Teaching Journal* 8, 2 (1983), pp. 10–15, 21–27. Argues for the importance of integrating thinking and intuitive styles in training models for management.

Carroll, Jerry. "Over-Achievers Swarm to This Exotic Class: MBA's Who Meditate, Chant and Read Tarot Cards." *San Francisco Chronicle* (February 17, 1983), p. 46. Tells more about the Ray and Myers class noted above.

Cates, Camille. "Beyond Muddling: Creativity." *Public Administration Review* (November–December 1979), pp. 527–32. Argues for an integrative approach to management that includes intuition.

Colligan, Douglass. "Your Gift of Prophecy." *Reader's Digest* (September 1982), pp. 145–50. Discusses the use of group intuition to predict the future.

Crawford, C. C., and John W. Demidovich. "Think Tank Technology for Systems Management." *Journal of Systems Management* (November 1981), pp. 22–25. Outlines the advantages of using the Crawford Slip Method for brainstorming and problem–solving situations to solicit input. Particularly useful technique with intuitive executives.

Denhardt, Robert E. "Managerial Intuition." *MBA* (February–March 1979), pp. 13–19. Discusses the importance of intuition in key management decisions.

Egerton, John. "Workers Take Over the Store." *New York Times* (September 11, 1983), pp. 164ff. We have the potential within our organizations if we will only set about to channel this talent to our mutual benefit. A good piece to show how using intuition can serve to increase productivity.

Engelmayer, Paul A. "Worker Owned and Operated Supermarket Yields Financial Success, Personal Rewards." *Wall Street Journal* (August 18, 1983), p. 23. Highly recommended for those who wish to not only increase productivity but also enhance the spirit of the place in which they work.

Everett, Ed. "Improving Creativity—One Organization's Approach." *Public Management* 65, 2 (February 1983), pp. 7–8. This government organization worked on developing their mental capital through the use of the Raudsepp book series.

Feinberg, Mortimer R., and Aaron Levenstein. "How Do You Know When to Rely on Your Intuition?" *Wall Street Journal* (June 21, 1982), p. 16. Gives examples of executive use and hints on how and when to use it.

"The Fine Art of Corporate Motivation." *New York Times* (September 11, 1983), p. F2. This article excerpt from the book *High Output Management* (New York: Harper & Row, 1983) by Andrew S. Grove, the president of INTEL Corporation, emphasizes the use of many of the basic principles of intuitive management.

Harman, Willis W. "This 20-Year Present." *Public Management* (January–February 1980), pp. 4–7. Explains why intuition will be more important in future management.

Herrmann, Ned. "The Brain and Management Learning." *Bureaucrat* (Fall 1982), pp. 17–21. Describes his whole brain approach to learning and creativity in management.

Holusha, John. "Toyota on G.M. Deal: Giving Aid to Opponent." *New York Times* (March 17, 1983), pp. 1, 36. Shows how the East and West view management from different thinking style perspectives.

Hughey, Ann. "An Old Hand at Bendix Uses a Sense of Humor in Merger with Allied." *Wall Street Journal* (August 22, 1983), p. 1. This article illustrates that how well BSM styles merge will determine in part the success or failure of the project.

"An Interview with Joseph McKinney: Chairman and CEO, Tyler Corporation." *Travelhost Prosperity Series* (February 28, 1982), pp. 4–5. This executive describes his "stray bullet drills" and use of intuition to make decisions.

Klein, Heywood. "Firms Seek Aid in Deciphering Japan's Culture." *Wall Street Journal* (September 1, 1983), p. 1. Understanding your opposite type can make a difference in your business success. This article outlines how some major organizations are trying to bridge the gap.

Leavitt, Harold J. "Beyond the Analytical Manager." *California Management Journal* (Spring 1975), pp. 5–12. Talks about the important need for brain skills such as intuition.

———. "Beyond the Analytical Manager: Part II." *California Management Journal*

(Summer 1975), pp. 11–21. Continues his above article with a discussion of extrasensory perception and techniques used for getting in touch with this ability.

Lehner, Urban C. "Understanding the Japanese Character." *Wall Street Journal* (December 9, 1983), p. 24. This review of Jared Taylor's book is useful as it shows within that person the inherent conflicts existing between thinking and intuitive brain styles. It takes work to overcome.

Liversidge, Anthony. "The Professor Who Teaches Presidents." *Omni* (March 1985), pp. 74–76, 116–20. Interview with Edward De Bono, father of lateral thinking concepts, who probably has done more than any other single writer in recent years to further new ways of understanding how the brain may function. The interview is provocative—even for the most traditional thinker.

MacArthur, Loren. "Artificial Intelligence." *Southwest Airlines Magazine* (October 1985), pp. 84–89, 120–25. Interview with John Seely Brown, head of the artificial intelligence research laboratory at Xerox Corporation. He discusses in part the importance of intuition in his own work in this area.

Miller, George A. "Varieties of Intelligence." *New York Times Book Review* (December 25, 1983), pp. 5, 20. This book review discusses Howard Gardner's book *Frames of Mind*. Several of the human intellectual competencies that Gardner identifies are closely linked to intuitive ability. Organizations of all types are recommended to examine his work.

Moore, Kermit. "Round-Table Reasoning." *American Way* (June 1984), pp. 149–52. How you organize your meeting will clearly affect the input you receive—especially from an intuitive type. This article tells you how to organize based on your objective.

Nauton, Ena. "Brain Wars: Which Side Are You On? The Right Side Just Might Be a Life Saver." *Miami Herald* (February 20, 1983), Living Today section, pp. 1, 8. Summarizes the work on brain theory and my own workshop on intuitive management at the University of Miami and elsewhere across the country.

Nelson, Bryce. "Bosses Face Less Risk than the Bossed." *New York Times* (April 3, 1983), p. 9. Indicates how stress and intuition can be linked by occupational specialty and level of responsibility.

Pondy, Louis R. "Union of Rationality and Intuition in Management Action." In *The Executive Mind: New Insights on Managerial Thought and Action*, edited by Sivastva, Suresh and Associates. San Francisco: Jossey-Bass, 1983, pp. 169–91. Argues that rationality and intuition are not antithetical and that each of these primary human functions works most effectively in combination with the other. This is very similar to my thesis that intuitive management is the integrating of so-called left and right brain management skills.

Prince, George M. "Creative Meetings Through Power Sharing." *Harvard Business Review* (July–August 1972), pp. 47–54. How cooperation and support can work. Intuition tells you how.

———. "Putting the Other Half of the Brain to Work." *Training* (November 1978), reprint. Tells you how to tap into your intuitive brain skills.

"Putting Heart Back into the Business of Business." *Management Practice* (Spring 1977), pp. 1–4. Importance of liking your work and knowing what you like. Intuition certainly will not hurt.

Raudsepp, Eugene. "Trust That Hunch!" *Success* (August 1982), pp. 27–30. Proposes using intuition—it works.

Rose, Ragsdale. "Using Intuition in Board Room." *San Francisco Chronicle* (September 16, 1985), pp. C3–4. Discusses how Inferential Focus, a New York based consulting firm, uses intuitive processes as well as more traditional projection techniques to serve its clients to anticipate future trends.

Scott, Niki. "Secretary Must Organize Boss." Universal Press Syndicate (May 5, 1984). Good to read before trying the exercise in Chapter 5, "Supervisor–Subordinate."

Serrin, William. "Companies Widen Worker Role in Decisions." *New York Times* (January 15, 1984), pp. 1, 12. Discusses how sharing of decisions has resulted in improved performance at a number of firms.

"The Seven Frames of Mind." *Psychology Today* (June 1984), pp. 19–33. Discusses Howard Gardner's pioneering work on different intelligence capabilities we may have. Recommended reading and clearly linked to intuitive ability.

Sorenson, Ralph Z. "A Lifetime of Learning to Manage Effectively." *Wall Street Journal* (February 28, 1983), p. 30. Experienced executive tells what it takes to manage effectively. Being sensitive to differences helps.

Stephen, Beverly. "Search Aims for Secrets of Success." Tribune Company Syndicate (1982). Success is correlated with characteristics of an intuitive manager.

Taggart, William, and Daniel Robey. "Mind and Managers: On the Dual Nature of Human Information Processing and Management." *Academy of Management* 6, 2 (1981), pp. 187–95. Styles by occupation are discussed. Artists tend to be intuitive while technicians are thinkers. Urges dual brain teaching in management educational programs. In the next issue of the same magazine [6, 3 (1981), pp. 375–83], in "Measuring Managers' Minds: The Assessment of Style in Human Information Processing," the authors discuss ways of testing for thinking styles among managers.

Train, John. "How to Feel: The Tao Theory." *Money & Investments* (April 1983), Inferential Focus reprint. Describes some of the applications of intuition, and how to prepare yourself for these cues.

Van Oech, Roger. "The Mind as a Management Tool." *Public Management* (January 1982), pp. 7–12. Keys to opening the intuition are outlined.

Vaughan, Alan. "Intuition, Precognition, and the Art of Prediction." *Futurist* (June 1982), pp. 5–10. Describes many of the practical applications of intuition and recent research on psi phenomena. Also gives you exercises on how to practice your ability to see the future.

Vocino, Thomas, and Jack Rabin, eds. *Contemporary Public Administration*. New York: Harcourt Brace Jovanovich, 1981. This basic introduction to public management treats the importance of intuitive decision making and how it compares to the so-called rational and empirical models.

Weyrich, Noel. "Managing Intuition." *New Age Journal* (May 1984), pp. 14–17. Feature article on my workshops on the use of intuition in management—in this case, with specific application to higher education institutions.

Yoshihara, Nancy. "Japan's Strategies May Need Some Tuning to Work Here." *Los Angeles Times* (January 23, 1983), pt. V, p. 3. Discusses the Japanese approach to management, the latest books on the subject, and the broader structure in Japan that supports business development, such as a government support system. Concludes that some adjustments need to be made in both management and government in this country for Japanese management concepts to work fully here.

Audio-Visual Materials

Agor, Weston H. "Intuition at the Top: How Successful Executives Make Their Deci-
    sions." El Paso, TX: ENFP Enterprises, 1985. This is a one hour video tape
    presentation before Chamber of Commerce executives. Explains how highly in-
    tuitive executives make their decisions and how you can build your skills in this
    area, and finishes with questions and answers.
————. "Intuitive Decision Making, Cassette Tape Number 1955." San Francisco, CA:
    New Dimensions Radio, 1985. Discusses how top executives use intuition to make
    important decisions based on field research nationally.
————. "Intuitive Management." Long Beach, CA: UMS Television Productions, 1984.
    Personal interview on the television program "Quest Four" by Damien Simpson.
    Discusses latest research on the use of intuition by top executives, and practical
    use of this brain skill in management.
————. "Intuitive Management: What It Is and How to Develop Your Skill." El Paso,
    TX: ENFP Enterprises, 1985. One hour cassette tape that describes how top
    executives use intuition to make decisions, the practical uses of intuition in man-
    agement, and exercises for you to develop your own ability further.
————. "Using Intuition to Be More Effective at Work and in Your Personal Life."
    Glendale, CA: Walt Disney Enterprises, 1982. Two hour video tape based on
    presentation to Walt Disney Enterprises managers and staff in the Walt Disney
    Enterprises Forum series (August 12, 1982). Lecture style, including discussion
    of intuition test, how to use results, resources to consult, and how to develop
    your skill further. Includes a self-hypnosis exercise.
————. "Your Management Style and Using Your Intuition." El Paso, TX: ENFP
    Enterprises, 1983. This is a one hour video tape presentation before Chamber of
    Commerce executives. Covers management style testing, the use of intuition in
    management, and how to develop your skill, and finishes with questions and
    answers.

Advertisement

"Saab Car: A Car for the Left Side of Your Brain—A Car for the Right Side of Your
    Brain." *Wall Street Journal* (January 1982). Business Section, p. 14. One example
    of the practical use of integrated brain skills in advertising.

Other Resources

Brain–Mind Bulletin. Los Angeles, CA: Interface Press. A newsletter issued every three
    weeks on innovative brain research and application in organizations that are trans-
    forming the world around us.
ENFP Enterprises. El Paso, TX: ENFP Enterprises, Inc. Describes the services and
    products of this management consulting firm specializing in testing for intuitive
    skills and their practical use in organizational decision making.
New Age Journal. Brighton, MA. A monthly journal featuring articles on cutting edge
    applications emerging that are likely to affect our life. Intuition is a frequently
    featured topic.
New Dimensions Radio. San Francisco, CA. Regularly produces interviews for public

radio transmission nationally on intuition and many other topics related to it. These interviews are also available in cassette tape for purchase.

New Realities. San Francisco, CA: Bi-monthly magazine that succeeded the former *Psychic Magazine*. Usually has many of the latest psi related authors featured as well as good book reviews on this field.

Index

About the Author

WESTON H. AGOR is Professor and Director of the Master of Public Administration Program at the University of Texas, El Paso, and president of a management consulting firm. Cited in Who's Who in America, he is the author of *Intuitive Management: Integrating Left and Right Brain Management Skills*, and the test instrument, *Test Your Intuitive Powers: AIM Survey*.